tony sutherland

THE ~~PERFECT~~ GRACE MADE MARRIAGE

secrets to enduring love

Cover Art, Direction, Layout and Design by Michael Hamilton
www.mchcreative.com

FOREWORD

Having served for over 26 years in marriage ministry, I have studied many books on the subject. I can confidently say, I have never read one as healing and freeing as *The Grace Made Marriage*. Also, as someone who has experienced needs in my own marriage and family, I am extremely passionate about extending greater measures of Grace in our homes. Any marriage, at any stage will benefit from this amazing resource for couples and the wisdom God has given in these pages.

There is no one better I can think of to impart understanding on Grace in marriage than Tony Sutherland. Tony and his wife Sherri are gifts to the Body of Christ and they serve with strength, loyalty, and humility. Whether Tony is speaking, writing, or singing, his years of experience and the anointing on his life invokes a response. The recurring theme of this book inspires and motivates couples to remove unhealthy expectations in their marriages and grant each other the Grace to be all God created and called them to be.

In a time where marriages are under incredible distress, we desperately need to cultivate atmospheres of Grace in our families. In all my years of working with couples, I have never seen a time where so many Christian marriages are under attack. With financial pressure, porn addictions, and extra-marital affairs on the rise, it is critical that we embrace this revelation of Grace to bring restoration to marriages. Healthy marriages are essential to happy homes, vibrant churches, and flourishing communities.

In I Peter 3:7, we are reminded that God created and designed marriage so that we could be "heirs together in the grace of life." God intended marriage to be full of His love and grace. Thank you Tony and Sherri for being examples and champions of God's great Grace in your marriage and for being obedient to write this necessary and transformational book! As you read and apply these truths, you will no doubt encounter that same healing Grace in your life and your most important relationship on earth!

Rebecca Keener
Former Marriage Pastor
Free Chapel 2007-2016
Co-host The Christian View

CONTENTS

DEDICATION

This book is affectionately dedicated to my wife, Sherri. For the past 27 years, she has been Christ's example of unconditional love, enduring support, and relentless forgiveness. She has shown me what true love looks like and continues to give me all the Grace I will never deserve.

INTRODUCTION

OK, so here goes. This is my attempt to present a solid book about one of the most complicated subjects on the planet... Marriage! You might ask, what do I know about marriage? Well for starters, I've been married 27 years, and that counts for a great deal. Now, I'm no expert on marriage, but I am experienced at just being married. I'm also not an authority on the subject of love nor am I a certified marriage counselor with a degree in relational therapy. I'm simply in a relationship with the woman I love and have experienced both the highs and the lows that go along with 27 years of marriage. Through it all, I'm still learning how to live, love, and last with the one God gave me. In almost three decades that my wife and I have been married, all of those being in ministry, we have had numerous opportunities to spend time with and minister to many other couples. We've listened to their stories, celebrated their triumphs, shared their struggles, grieved over their losses, and then some. Yet, through it all, we've had the joy to encourage and help many couples go on to have strong and happy marriages. We've seen couples beautifully restored and now thriving all because of God's Grace..

So, in this book we're going to talk a lot about Grace. I'm going to show you that the way to have a lasting and fulfilling marriage is by giving and receiving Grace from God and for each other. You can't achieve love from God, you can only receive love. It's the same way in marriage. You cannot achieve a loving marriage. You can only receive it and live it out through the Grace of God. While marriage helps can be helpful, they don't solve the deeper problems in the marriage. By the way, Jesus didn't come to just fix our problems; he came to save us to the uttermost, to completely redeem and make us whole. The same is true for your marriage. Jesus didn't come to tweak your marriage, he came to totally revolutionize it and make it all it was meant to be.

This book wasn't written to give your marriage a *boost* or a temporary *fix*. This book is all about letting Christ be the center of your marriage and allowing his Grace to change everything. Grace truly makes a marriage all it can be. It forms a marriage, supports a marriage, keeps a marriage and if it's in trouble, completely saves a marriage. Whether your marriage is interstellar or whether it's on the tattered edge of unraveling; Grace is the answer! Grace rescued and redeemed you and it can do the same for your marriage. LOVE never fails. Christ never fails! If your marriage is good, it can be better. If your marriage is broken, Grace can fix it. That's a promise!

Today, so many couples give up and walk out. In fact, a recent survey taken by www.politifact.com suggests that the "overall probability of marriages now ending in divorce falls between forty and fifty percent."[20] Tragic! My sincere prayer is that through this book many couples will find insight, encouragement, hope, and joy for their marriages. After all, no marriage is perfect. That's why there's GRACE! God wants you to have the best marriage you ever thought possible. Although you may not have a perfect marriage, by God's Grace, you and your mate ARE perfect for each other. That's what a Grace made marriage is all about.

Chapter 1

GRACE IN MARRIAGE

Over the years, I've observed that couples, generally speaking, become more interested in reading a book about marriage or going to a marriage conference if a relational "expert" claims to possess the secret for a divorce-proof-marriage. Yet, there is no such resource out there that can truly guarantee a divorce-proof marriage. It simply does not exist. Rather, marriage is best lived out when Grace is the foundation and regularly applied. Grace in marriage... What does this mean? Overall it means that you should accept your mate with unconditional love, in spite of their sometimes misguided temperaments and despicable dispositions, with *no-guarantees* of fixing the flaws. In contrast, a Law-based marriage says if you do this or do that, if you meet my expectations and live up to my standards, then I will fully accept you. That's the way the Law works. Many couples live together with hidden reservations of yet fully accepting their mate. This only produces deep resentment which eventually seeps it's way out into the relationship, giving off a lingering air of bitterness. Suffocating! Couples can never fully inhale and exhale the air of freedom in this kind of environment.

The Law in essence tells us that our actions determine our outcomes. In other words, we get what we deserve. Yet, by Grace we got what Jesus deserved, and Jesus got what we deserved. And there's more. Grace says the less we deserve God's love the more we receive it. This concept totally applies to marriage. The less your mate deserves love, the more you should give it. God is rich in love towards us the same way, and so should we be toward one another in marriage (Ephesians 2:4-5). Through Christ we receive this kind of love not only at the onset of our salvation, but throughout our entire relationship with Him. Underserved love! God does not give us Grace just upon salvation and then place us back under the system of the Law to earn His acceptance. No! We live under the canopy of His amazing Grace at all times (Song of Solomon 2:4). This same Grace enables us to live, breathe and soar in marriage. How can we not love someone back who loves us this way? Under a Grace made marriage, we not only promise to love unconditionally upon our marriage vows, but truly until death do us part, good times and bad. When you truly know your mate unconditionally loves you, it removes the pressure to perform and frees you to love without limitations. Just as we feel completely secure in Christ's love, so husbands and wives should feel in each other's love. Grace teaches us how to truly love. The key to fully loving your mate unconditionally is to freely receive Christ's love for yourself. As you receive Christ's love, you are able to love your spouse in the same way.

> **"A new command I give you; Love one another. AS I HAVE LOVED YOU, so you must love one another." (John 13:34 NIV)**

When Grace is at the center of marriage, couples can wholeheartedly and genuinely love each other in spite of their differences and shortcomings. And since we are on this subject of Grace in marriage, it is important to understand the one foundational truth of Grace; and that is we cannot earn our righteousness. It is the free gift of God and can be received only by Grace (Romans 6:23). In no way can we attribute our salvation to our own efforts or boast of our ability to maintain it (Ephesians 2:8-9). The same is true in marriage. Marriage is a gift from God. You didn't deserve your mate, but God gave them to you anyway. You must view your marriage as a free gift from God. My wife is a representation of God's gift of Grace. When we view our spouses as God's gift of Grace, that same Grace will begin to work powerfully in our marriages. Important note: Grace is not just basic leniency, temporary slack or momentary forgiveness until we get *it* right. Grace is the complete, comprehensive, 100% full pardon of God based solely of the work and sufficiency of Jesus. It is given without reservation or hesitation. This is exactly how we should give and receive love in marriage. When couples exchange this kind of undeserved and unreserved Grace, it creates a deep sense of intimacy in the relationship. A great marriage flows from true intimacy not instructions. It is founded on love not lists. Many couples are constantly looking for something to measure their relationship by. It's give me more tools, more tips, more trends, and more techniques. The problem is these things (although not bad in and of themselves) can eventually create standards we use to measure each other by. This is how the Law operates. The Law demands perfect performance. However, the Law is never satisfied no matter how good our performance. When we live out of performance-based expectations in marriage, we will never be truly satisfied with one another, because the Law is never satisfied. Your good works or "perfect" performance are never good enough. Thus, is the cycle of a Law-based marriage. Grace is always accepting, loving, understanding, receiving, and gracious while the Law is always heavy, rude, demanding, irritable, pressuring, forceful, angry, and nagging. The Bible doesn't suggest that the nagging wife convinces the husband or the demanding husband changes the wife. Rather, it states that the believing wife sanctifies the husband and vice versa (1 Corinthians 7:14). Pride prevents us from seeing the work God is doing in our marriage and in our spouses. When we don't see certain changes on our own timetable we tend to pressure and manipulate one another. Again, this is the Law at work in the marriage. However, Grace reminds us to rest while the Holy Spirit is at work. When you work,

Grace rests, but when you rest, Grace works. By grace, through faith, you must trust that your spouse is daily coming into the fullness of all God has designed them to be. Resist placing expectations of perfection upon your mate in this life. It will only cause painful disappointment on a regular basis. By Grace, God sees us through the finished work of His Son. Likewise, we must see our spouses shining in that same radiant light. As I have stated, the Law-based marriage insists perfect performance. However, while the Law demands; Grace supplies. Therefore a marriage that trusts in the Grace of God will be supplied with all it needs to become all it should.

All throughout marriage you will have the opportunity to be tempted to think your mate is lacking and less than what they should be. Only through Christ can you see your spouse as totally righteous before God, complete, and lacking nothing (Colossians 2:10). Through Grace we can continue to believe in our spouses no matter what we see manifesting on the outward (2 Corinthians 5:7).

Another essential aspect of a Grace made marriage is understanding how God views us. God's perspective is the single most important factor in relation to how we experience joy in our lives. On an individual basis, if we have a skewed perspective of how God relates to us, we will constantly struggle to experience his joy, peace and freedom. Likewise, couples often struggle the most in marriage when they have a distorted perception of one another. Couples must see each another in the exact same light as God sees us: exactly like his Son, without spot or wrinkle. We are the righteousness of God in Christ.

**"God made him who had no sin to be sin
for us, so that in him we might
become the righteousness of God."
(2 Corinthians 5:21 NIV)**

Did you see that? We are the righteousness OF GOD. This means if your spouse is born again, then they are as righteous AS GOD. When we allow Grace to govern the way we see ourselves and view our spouses, transformation is imminent. Growth in marriage is possible when couples resist pointing at one another's failures and instead believe they are all God says they are, speaking kindly and generously of one another. We should say things like, *"I love the way Christ is working in you." "I believe that God's plan is working in your favor." "I love you no matter what."*

The Law predicates performance based on demands. It's, do it my way or the highway. I heard a song once with a lyric that said, *"I want to love you like I'm losing you."* This type of love is founded on the fear of losing the other. This is Law at work in marriage. However, Christ confidently sets the record straight: *"I will never, abandon you, walk away, turn my eyes, deviate my course, break my promises, or forsake you,"* (Hebrews 13:5). It is from Christ's unwavering commitment that we receive inspiration for our marriages. Too many couples feel the underlying current of pressure to change for their mate. They dread the outcome of rejection, so couples do everything to ensure that rejection never happens. Fear is the motivator. It's like the Johnny Cash song—So many couples live in paranoia that their marriage is doomed to fail unless they *walk the line*. However, our relationship with God doesn't work like this. Through the work of Christ, God has completely removed the fear of abandonment based on performance?

"There is no fear in love, but perfect love casts out fear; for fear has torment, and he that fears has not been made perfect in love."
(1 John 4:18 NIV)

There is NO fear in love and there should be no fear in marriage. God has completely removed fear from the equation of our salvation. It's tormenting to think that God would abandon us if we fail to meet all His expectations. Yet, the kingdom of God is not founded on fear, but righteousness, peace and joy in the Holy Spirit (Romans 14:17). When we see each other as totally and completely righteous, it produces a peace in our relationship which, in turn, opens the door for abundant joy to reign in our marriages. It is through an abundance of Grace that our marriages will thrive (Romans 5:17). Under Grace we don't fear failure, rather we believe in hope. This only produces every good thing in marriage. Even one ounce of fear of what the other will do based on our performance has the potential to gnaw away at our relationships like a termite. However, when you know there is no reason to fear in your relationship with God it will produce unflinching loyalty and faithfulness to Him and at the same time, fidelity towards one another. When Grace is at the center of a relationship it holds all things and pulls all things together. True devotion flows from effortless love supplied by Grace. I am not faithful to my wife because I am afraid of her, but because I deeply love her and that love originates from God. Expressed love is a natural byproduct of Grace. Love is the motivator here!

When fear is the motivating factor in a relationship, it produces pressure on the other person to change. However, true change doesn't come from fear-pressure. Rather, it is birthed from a sense of peace. We have a hard enough time trying to change ourselves more or less attempting to change our spouses. You will only frustrate your marriage when you attempt to manipulate your spouse to change. It's unrealistic and simply impossible. You cannot force your mate to become what you want them to be. You must believe in who they already are and trust God with the rest. The life of Grace is a spirit FILLED life not a spirit FORCED life. You can't force your spouse to be fruitful in love and Godliness any more than you can force an apple tree to grow apples. The key is to water the tree and point it in the direction of the sun. The same is true of your marriage. You can't nag, urge, scream, or demand that your mate produce the fruit of the spirit and qualities of becoming a righteous, loving, and faithful mate. You must believe that God has already made them perfect by His Grace and continue to sow faith, hope, and love into the relationship. Your mate will not manifest spiritual fruit through your natural urging. Spiritual fruit is something only the Holy Spirit can produce. That's why it's called the fruit of the SPIRIT.

Grace must be the foundation in order for couples to experience the full liberty that God intended in marriage. The purity of God's Grace motivates all efforts made in the relationship. It's not, *"I do for you to make you love me."* Rather It's, *"I do for you because you love me and because I love you."* Grace is the inspiration for all effective endeavors in marriage. The primary foundation of Grace is the finished work of Christ. Again, we are not saved by our own works (Ephesians 2:7-9). However, Grace in marriage is not opposed to applying effort in marriage. It takes a great deal of effort for a relationship to be all it can be. Grace isn't opposed to works; it's opposed to earning. The problem with many marriages is husbands and wives are still trying to *earn* favor with one another. That is a grueling cycle. However, while earning is not the basis of a good marriage, a great marriage does take effort. Effort is simply taking action in marriage. Grace in marriage does not imply laziness, apathy, lethargy, passivity, or negligence (1 Corinthians 15:10). When Grace is fully at play in marriage, couples will take the necessary action to work on their marriage without anxiety and pressure; and do whatever it takes, for as long as it takes. Great marriages do not evade good marriage practice or abandon sound moral principles. You and your mate can make it through life's challenges and changes if you decide from the start, come what may, to do whatever it takes for your marriage to succeed.

Finally, Grace holds a marriage together when both you and your mate are changing and growing, even though each of you may not be growing and changing into the person you used to know. Life has a way of changing us. When you first start out as a couple you have all these expectations of what you want your marriage to become and what you're going to conquer together. Then after a few years, unexpected storms arise, surprise twists and turns unfold, and we are tempted to allow dissolution and disappointment to settle in. Yet, through all of life's changes, Grace weathers every storm. It's amazing how the Grace of God has enabled Sherri and I to make transition through some very difficult seasons of our marriage. Grace has helped us to accept the changes and challenges that have come and yet still fiercely love one another through it all. In the course of your marriage you will go through seasons. You will make changes in your careers, passions, interests, and even temperaments. You will never stop discovering your giftings and who you are. You may not see the changes coming in one another. Yet, if you allow Grace to be at the center of your relationship, you are in for an *amazing adventure.*

Chapter 2

WHAT LOVE LOOKS LIKE

There's a classic rock song from the 1980's entitled "Love Hurts." Many claim that love hurts; but actually love doesn't hurt. Rejection hurts. Failing relationships hurt. Losing someone you thought would be "the one" hurts. Let's not get the bad things that happen in a relationship confused with love. True love is the one single thing in life that doesn't hurt. Love is what makes life and relationships wonderful. The reason why some say love hurts is because they *feel* hurt, and after all, feeling good is what keeps a relationship together, isn't it? Not so! Some think love is some magical feeling. Love isn't a feeling. Love produces feelings, but the core of love isn't a feeling. Love is the living essence of God. God is pure love (1 John 4:8) and God's perfect love is reflected in His choice to die for us even while we were sinners. Christ didn't just die for the "good guy" (as if there are any really good). He also died for the criminal, the murderer, the thief, the despicable, and the worst of the worst.

"For one will hardly die for a righteous man; though perhaps for the good man someone would dare even to die. But God demonstrates His own love toward us, in that while we were yet sinners, Christ died for us."
(Romans 5:7-8 NASB)

None of us, without God's Grace working deeply in us, could demonstrate love in this way. Look at how THE MESSAGE translations renders this same verse.

"We can understand someone dying for a person worth dying for, and we can understand how someone good and noble could inspire us to selfless sacrifice. But God put his love on the line for us by offering his Son in sacrificial death while we were of no use whatever to him." (Romans 5:7-8 MSG)

Perfect love can only be exemplified by a perfect God. God's love was a choice, an action, a purpose to save us and stay with us in spite of our rebellion and sin. That kind of love is the full reflection of His Grace, and in spite of our continued struggle with sin, He will still never abandon or disown us. God's perfect love is infallibly consistent even when we are miserably inconsistent (2 Timothy 2:13).

Christian couples must remember that even though they are born again and have a new nature, they still live in the earthly realm and at best, mostly demonstrate love that is limited by natural elements. God's love is completely supernatural and only by allowing that kind of love to supernaturally flow through us can we display it to one another in marriage. Simply put, true love in marriage can only be demonstrated by God's Grace through his Spirit. *God is the only true and pure essence of love.* His love is absolutely perfect. Yet, the amazing thing is that a perfectly loving God has merged Himself with our frail and faulty humanity. While God's love is perfect, the truth is people don't perfectly show God's love to one another. All it takes is one good reading of 1 Corinthians 13 to prove that not one human being alive loves perfectly.

"If I speak in the tongues of men or of angels, but do not have love, I am only a resounding gong or a clanging cymbal. If I have the gift

of prophecy and can fathom all mysteries and all knowledge, and if I have a faith that can move mountains, but do not have love, I am nothing. If I give all I possess to the poor and give over my body to hardship that I may boast, but do not have love, I gain nothing. Love is patient, love is kind. It does not envy, it does not boast, it is not proud. It does not dishonor others, it is not self-seeking, it is not easily angered, it keeps no record of wrongs. Love does not delight in evil but rejoices with the truth. It always protects, always trusts, always hopes, always perseveres. Love never fails… And now these three remain: faith, hope and love. But the greatest of these is love." (1 Corinthians 13:1-13 NIV)

It is a mistake to assume that couples are capable of always exercising and demonstrating perfect love. Only God's love is divine, beyond imagination, and unfathomable to the human mind. We must settle this. All too often we put false expectations on our mates to love us on the same level as God: consistently, perfectly, flawlessly. God alone is altogether lovely, flawless, radiant, and majestic. Yet somehow when couples get married they think their love will be perpetual angelic bliss. And so it goes, when couples fail at love, they condemn one another and even blame love. Again, what is to blame? Is it love, or is it the person attempting to demonstrate love. Couples set themselves up for failure and disappointment when they judge the imperfect love of one another against the perfect Love of God. Even more tragic, when people get hurt or disappointed in their relationships, they begin to shut off their feelings. They become emotionally seared. So many couples are trapped in a cycle of bitterness. They have decided not to allow themselves to be hurt again and again, so they avoid reconciliation and restoration altogether.

1 Corinthians 13 has been quoted, taught, preached and taped on refrigerators everywhere to show married couples how to be better at love. Yet, this passage is not being used by Paul for this purpose. 1 Corinthians 13 wasn't written to tell us *how* to love, but rather to illustrate what perfect love is. Paul is known as the apostle of Grace (Acts 20:24). Therefore, everything we read from Paul's writings must be seen through the lens of Grace. His sole purpose for writing 1 Corinthians 13 was to paint the picture of Christ's perfect love. It isn't the superficial kind of love that is based off of feelings but rather based off of a firm commitment to love with the same kind of Love that Christ has for us.

The Old Covenant Law demanded that we love God perfectly, not based on our standard but on his perfect standard. A similar statement in the New Testament was when Jesus said, *"You have heard it said not to murder. But I say to you don't be angry with your brother or you are guilty of the same."* (Matthew 5:21-22 My Paraphrase). Here Jesus introduced Law 2.0 to show us that living by the Law is impossible. Paul similarly illustrates God's perfect love in 1 Corinthians 13 to show us in essence that we are incapable of giving this kind of love apart from His grace. However, even then, we still cannot love perfectly at all times. Thus, couples that demand and expect perfect love from each other will eventually be disappointed to some degree.

Another passage similar to 1 Corinthians 13 that demonstrates God's love even takes it a step further. Christ's love is used as an example to teach us love and submission in the marriage relationship.

"Submit to one another out of reverence for Christ. Wives, submit yourselves to your own husbands as you do to the Lord. For the husband is the head of the wife as Christ is the head of the church, his body, of which he is the Savior. Now as the church submits to

Christ, so also wives should submit to their husbands in everything. Husbands, love your wives, just as Christ loved the church and gave himself up for her to make her holy, cleansing her by the washing with water through the word, and to present her to himself as a radiant church, without stain or wrinkle or any other blemish, but holy and blameless. In this same way, husbands ought to love their wives as their own bodies. He who loves his wife loves himself. After all, no one ever hated their own body, but they feed and care for their body, just as Christ does the church—for we are members of his body. "For this reason a man will leave his father and mother and be united to his wife, and the two will become one flesh." 32 This is a profound mystery—but I am talking about Christ and the church. However, each one of you also must love his wife as he loves himself, and the wife must respect her husband. (Ephesians 5:21-33 NIV)

No one is entirely capable of perfectly giving this kind of love. After all, at the core of our being we are selfish, self centered, egotistical, proud, arrogant, boastful, stingy, temperamental and so much more. The question begs to be asked, if no one is perfect at love then how is it possible to love in marriage? This is the defining theme of this book. Applying Grace in marriage doesn't make a marriage perfect. Grace should be applied because NO marriage is perfect. *Thus, a Grace made marriage is one that allows Grace to be the center of the marriage thereby working THROUGH us to demonstrate God perfect love to one another.* Love is the essence of marriage. In spite of all our shortcomings to love perfectly, we should make an attempt to love anyway. We aren't judged by God if we love imperfectly. Rather our marriages are strengthened when we attempt to love regardless of our inability to love perfectly.

You may have heard it said and accepted among most, that a strong relationship is built on trust. This is true to a certain degree. However, a relationship is not totally built on trust. In fact, we are instructed not to put our trust in man (Psalms 146:3; Isaiah 2:22). This means even our mates. It is presumptuous to think our spouses will not fail us. Yet, we go into our marriages subconsciously believing this to be true. God is the only one we can stake all our trust in. For this reason, Jesus commanded us to simply LOVE one another (John 15:12). The love my wife and I have for each other is not founded solely upon trust, but more fully on our unconditional love for one another as God demonstrates it through us. Our love is faulty, but his love alone is perfect. If couples open their hearts and allow God's perfect love to flow through them, they can love each other through the most difficult of times. The strongest marriages, the ones that last through seasons of disappointment and disillusionment of broken trust, are the ones that have made a steadfast choice to love each other no matter what. A lasting marriage is built on the solid foundation of God's love. We are to put all our trust in God and simply love one another. Trust is indeed one of the pillars of the marriage relationship. However, while trust is a pillar; LOVE is the foundation. While couples may not always be able to trust one another, they can always choose to love one another with the unconditional love that only comes from God as it's source. People fail. Spouses fail, sometimes in small ways and other times in colossal ways. The problem with many marriages is that they place all their trust in each other to meet one another's needs when only God is capable of meeting their needs.

"And my God will meet all your needs according to the riches of his glory in Christ Jesus." (Philippians 4:19 NIV).

This includes all our spiritual, physical, and emotional needs. Even our deepest needs for approval, acceptance, and forgiveness can only be met in Christ. We can receive these things from each other in marriage only in part, but the totality of who we are can only be satisfied in Christ. When we seek to find total satisfaction in our mates, we wind up disappointed and even disillusioned. Only when we love each other out of a base of finding our acceptance and deep emotional approval in Christ, can we truly love one another. That's why Jesus instructed us to love one another AS he loves us. When we receive love and Grace from Christ we are empowered to love one another out of the well spring of Christ's love.

"Love one another. As I have loved you, so you must love one another." (John 13:34 NIV)

The truth is, couples cannot love one another with the perfect and unconditional love of Christ unless they regularly receive his love on an individual basis. We can only truly demonstrate Christ love AS he pours his love into us. As a result, over time, a couple's love for one anther will more fully reflect the reality of Christ's love. We are not commanded to love perfectly; we are simply called to love, and as we do, God's love is continually perfected through us.

"If we love one another, God abides in us and his love is perfected in us." (1 John 4:12 ESV)

When you said "I Do" upon your marriage vows, you were simply saying you would do your best to unconditionally love your mate and fulfill your promises as long as you live. When you fully decide to love in spite of your mate's failures, to stay in it no matter the difficulty, when you make a decision that for the rest of your life you're going to unconditionally love this other person that God brought into your life, Christ's love finds a way to make your marriage thrive. Grace finds a way to help a marriage last through the harshest of times.

Sometime 1 Corinthians 13 and Ephesians 5:21-33 can be difficult passages to read because we all have failed at love. However, failing at love doesn't mean we're not loving; it simply means we're learning to love. That pain in our hearts that we feel when we fail our spouses; you know, that scalding hot lava rock that sits in the pit of our stomachs… That's love trying to happen. That's love trying to work itself out in our lives. The pain of failing at love is the catalyst for learning to love. It's selfishness squeezing it's way out of our hearts. These passages weren't meant to show us how to love. They were meant to show us how imperfect we are at loving in the luminescence of Christ's perfectly radiant love. Although no one but Jesus can give this kind of love, these passages can show us a model of love.

Sometimes it seems we could fulfill our Biblical role as spouses much easier if our mates would simply do what they are called to do. If they would cultivate a stronger prayer life, we would feel better about them. If they were growing in their walk with Christ, we would be honored to submit to them and love them. If they truly loved as Christ loved the church, then we would shower them with respect.[1] Yet, our calling to love in marriage doesn't hinge upon how faithfully our mates walk out their obedience to God. We stand before the Lord alone, and we do all as unto him. I know it is tempting to focus on where your mate are lacking—especially when that someone lives under the same roof, with habits and idiosyncrasies you've dissected for years.[1] It's easy for couples to become nit-picky and critical about where their spouses need to be and all the while overlook the numerous shortcomings in their own lives. Oh, and if their love is lacking, it's downright heartbreaking. How do we set aside our own hurt and frustration and live out the love that the scriptures lay out for us? How do we walk together when the other is lacking and not adequately fulfilling their role in the marriage?[1] These are real issues, ones I must admit that I fall short of. Yet, I can only love and do my best to walk in something that Christ can only teach me by His perfect love. We can serve one another, pray for each other, give our best to each other, encourage one another, submit to one another, and the like. However, we must realize that these are not full-proof rules for a perfect marriage. They are simply helps as we attempt to love and display Grace toward our mates and grow in the same kind of love that Christ gives.[1]

During our 27 years of marriage my wife and I have been to several marriage retreats and conferences, read a lot of books and listened to a variety of speakers tell us how to make our marriage better. Some of this has encouraged us along the way and given us a temporary shot in the arm for a season. However, the best thing we have ever done in our marriage is continue to walk out our commitment to love in every season and in every circumstance. We've found that love really works. Faithful love is the essence of God's

Grace. Unconditional love! Our marriage has suffered the greatest setbacks when we focused on the pain and disappointment we have caused each other by not living up to each other's standards and fulfilling the promises we have made to each other. Love in marriage cancels out the laws of marriage. This is the essence of Law and Grace. When Grace is applied, no law can break it and no law can build upon it (Galatians 5:23). Simply put, a Grace made marriage is built on Christ's love; nothing more, nothing less.

It's one thing to talk about love, but what does it look like? Love looks like something. Love is displayed in our actions and how we treat one another. Love to me looks like a plate full of pancakes on a cold Saturday winter morning. You know they say the way to a man's heart is through his stomach. To my wife, love looks like a massage table set up in our room after a long difficult day at work. To me love sounds like words of affirmation from my wife that I am still "the man," that I am her hero, the one who is the best preacher, the best writer, and the best singer than anyone in the world. To my wife love sounds like a soft gentle tone in my voice and words of kindness spoken to her and the kids. Love to my wife looks like trimming back the bushes before winter and taking care of the cars when they need servicing. My wife doesn't demand these things and still loves me when they don't get done, but I love seeing the smile on her face when I do them. These are small things that add up to a lot in a loving relationship. When we love like Christ we are demonstrating his Grace. Christ didn't just say he loved us. He proved his love to us through action. He left everything for us. He didn't come demanding anything. He won our hearts with his sacrificial love. He demonstrated undeserved love and unconditional Grace (Romans 5:8).

God's love and Grace remain unconditional in spite of our imperfect ability to reciprocate that love. God knows our human love is flawed, but His love remains perfect towards us. His love for us is not dependent on our *performance;* it is dependent on His *promise.* God loves us without reservation, expectation, stipulation, or conditions. When we focus on God's promises to us we will naturally grow deeper in love with Him and develop a heartfelt desire to walk in obedience and keep His commandments. We don't keep God's commandments to get His love. God's love works in us to help us keep His commandments.[3] This is how the Grace made marriage works. Unconditional love for one another fuels our hearts to love each other unconditionally. Obligatory love never gets the desired results. While demanding may produce compliance it never produces a genuine response. There are many times that I don't deserve my wife's love, yet I've noticed over the years that she continues to demonstrate love to me many times in undeserved ways. Throughout our marriage, my wife and I have tried the hands-on-the-hips, demanding type attitude. However, we've both discovered it mostly backfires. However, when we respond graciously to each other when we don't deserve it, it isn't too long that the tension of unforgiveness, bitterness, and anger melt away. Many times I've deserved reprimand and scolding. However, when my wife has displayed love, regardless of my behavior, it made me realize what a *jerk* I was and it aptly moved my heart to respond in loving action. For instance, on days when I am grumpy or irritable (legitimate or not), when my wife grants understanding and freedom for me to have bad days, it makes it easier for me to confront my attitude with honesty. Conversely, it's when she tells me in her frustration that I'm being irritable, that it only makes me more irritable.

Under the Law, we struggle to be free but under Grace, we are free to struggle. In other words, there are seasons when I'm struggling with my own insecurities, short comings and failures and don't get things right but God's Grace is still for me. *The Grace made marriage makes huge allowances for each other's issues.* We shouldn't make constant demands that our mate get things right. Rather we should trust that God, in his time, will work out the inconsistencies in one another. Our commitment to love one another through our bad days provides the room to grow, make adjustments and overcome the things that hold us back in life. Rather than corner one another with an iron fist of intimidation, husbands and wives should stand in each other's corner and cheer one another on with encouragement, affirmation, love and Grace. It's in the times when we are falling short that we should stand tall for each other. The only time we should look down on one another is when we are attempting to help one another up. Again, we will never love as perfectly as Christ has loved us this side of Heaven, but we can continue to grow in our love for each other here on earth as we continually demonstrate it. We should never use the excuse that because we are not perfect, we can't still try at love.

Christ has liberally poured his love in our hearts (Romans 5:5). As we love one another, the love that Christ put in our hearts actually has somewhere to go. Love is always looking for an outlet. Jesus gives his love to us so that he can love through us, and He would never ask of us anything that he knows we are not able to do by his Grace. Because of the love Christ has given us, we are more than capable of reflecting that love toward one another. When we demonstrate what love looks like, not only do we fulfill God's purpose for our marriages all the more, but we also enjoy our marriages all the more.

Chapter 3

LOVING IS SERVING

A woman takes her husband to the doctor's office. He has been struggling with heart problems and many physical ailments preventing him from enjoying his life. The woman waits in the waiting room while the doctor examines the husband. After the examination, he sends the man back into the waiting room and calls the wife in. He tells the wife that most of her husband's problems stem from working too hard. He continues to tell her that if she wants her husband to live longer, she will need to let him rest on the couch everyday for the next several months. He is not to do any heavy lifting, yard work, painting, or any odds and ends repair jobs. He is simply to lay back on the couch, relax and watch TV. The doctor instructs her not to bring any extra stress into the home nor irritate or agitate him in anyway. She is to cook him three square meals and do anything extra he asks of her. She must bring him all his meals and not allow him to get off the couch unless absolutely necessary. The doctor tells her that if she doesn't abide by these procedures exactly as he has prescribed, her husband probably won't live much longer. The woman thanks the doctor and the couple checks out. During the ride home the husband is confused. He doesn't understand why the doctor didn't talk to him. He then asks his wife, *"What did the doctor say to you?"* The wife replies, *"You are surely going to die!"*

Serving one another in marriage sometimes isn't fun and for those who do more of the giving in the marriage, it can become a constant chore. It is important to remember in the Grace made marriage that serving isn't the way we earn love from one another, but it is surely the way we SHOW love in the marriage. Everyone appreciates when others show love in practical ways (i.e. gifts, acts of service, emotional expression, physical touch, affection, etc.). Jesus instructed the disciples how to demonstrate love.

"Jesus knew that the Father had put all things under his power, and that he had come from God and was returning to God; so he got up from the meal, took off his outer clothing, and wrapped a towel around his waist. After that, he poured water into a basin and began to wash his disciples' feet, drying them with the towel that was wrapped around him... When he had finished washing their feet, he put on his clothes and returned to his place.

"Do you understand what I have done for you?" he asked them. "You call me 'Teacher' and 'Lord,' and rightly so, for that is what I am. Now that I, your Lord and Teacher, have washed your feet, you also should wash one another's feet. I have set you an example that you should do as I have done for you. Very truly I tell you, no servant is greater than his master, nor is a messenger greater than the one who sent him. Now that you know these things, you will be blessed if you do them."
(John 13:3-17 NIV)

Jesus was the most powerful man in the room and yet he used his power not to Lord-over but to serve under. The scriptures are very clear that Husbands are to love their wives even as Christ loved the church (Ephesians 5:25). Here Jesus shows love in action by serving! I know many men won't like to hear this, but often the degree that you serve is the degree that you love. Why doesn't the Bible say for women to serve. Because serving is in their DNA. Let's be honest. Who typically does more serving in the marriage? The woman. Let's not debate it. I'm not saying it's this way in every marriage, but for the most part, women have a more serving demeanor. I don't know too many men who do all the cooking, laundry, house cleaning, care giving for children, nursing, etc. The Bible doesn't say that women should serve their husbands. It says they should submit to their husbands.

The Bible doesn't say that we have to love serving but we do have to lovingly serve to demonstrate our love. Simply put, we prove our love for one another by serving one another. Jesus washed the disciples feet. Think how dirty their feet were. They didn't wear socks and the streets were made of dirt. It was bare feet on dirt roads. Jesus silences every voice of entitlement by his loving act to wash his disciples feet. Sometimes in marriage we feel entitled to be served. Entitlement is a symptom of self-righteousness. It's, "I've done all *this* for you and the least you could do is do *that* for me." Self-righteousness at the very core says, *"Because I've done this then I deserve this.*" But Grace says we deserve nothing from Christ no matter what you've done but he gives us everything anyway. In marriage our service towards one another isn't based on how well or how much our mate has done. Our service to them is based on Christ love for us and our love for THEM. In fact, it's the goodness of God that leads us toward submission and loving service. Husbands, if you want your wife to submit to you, don't lord over them in a demanding way. Show them you love them by giving to them in sacrificial ways. You might say, I thought Grace was God's undeserved favor and that we don't earn his love by our works. That is true. We are not in anyway saved by works but we are saved UNTO works. The scriptures tell us that by doing good works, the world will see them and it will bring glory to God.

"Let your light shine before others, that they may see your good deeds and glorify your Father in heaven." (Matthew 5:16 NIV)

The same applies to our marriage. We don't earn love by doing good works for one another, but we *show* love by doing good works for each other. In turn we will see the glory of God working in our marriage. When I serve my wife I get the opportunity for her to see God's love for her on display. His love works through me as I serve her and by this she is more affectionately drawn to him through me. My service to my wife is not ultimately to win her love but to turn her love toward God. I am serving to draw her to the Love of Christ. By my example, I show her the Grace of God. Grace is a verb. Grace is Christ in action through me. When I serve the needs of my wife, I become a channel for God to fulfill his promise to supply my wife's needs according to his riches. When I am rich in love through serving, my wife more fully comes to understand the love of Christ. Of course all of this applies as my wife serves me as well. No one in the marriage is exempt from the privilege to serve. The scriptures instruct us in this way so that we will become the beneficiaries of love both through giving and receiving.

Some may tell you that marriage is 50/50; that it's give and take. That is not entirely true. Marriage is 100/100. It is ALL giving. It is unrealistic for me to expect my wife to give. Even though it's reasonable to desire it, it doesn't mean its inevitable. That is the risk of serving. Just because I serve doesn't mean my wife will serve me back in the same measure. If I expect her to return the "favor" and she doesn't, it opens the door for disappointment. But Grace doesn't give expecting to receive. Christ died for me when I was powerless to give anything back (Romans 5:7-9). That's what makes it Grace. Couples should display this type of grace in serving. In this way, both will not just receive 50% but 100% from each other. The more both partners in the marriage give, it is reasonable to believe we can live in the fullest pleasure of giving and receiving from each other.

Sometimes we serve our mates halfheartedly because we feel they are prone to do all the receiving. I call this cheap service. It's, *"I'm holding back because you are holding back."* However, when we serve with this kind of reservation we neutralize the power of Grace in our marriages. Grace isn't cheap; it's free, and we must serve one another freely and liberally and trust the Lord to work in the heart of the other. God is in charge of all the outcomes of our service. We can only serve and leave everything else in the hands of God. Obedience to God to serve doesn't come with obligations on the part of our mate. We simply obey God to serve. Our serving must not be preempted with ulterior motives or the other will sense it and our serving will lose it's effectiveness. We must take on the heart of Christ when we serve one another. His heart was to seek, serve, and save with no strings attached. Our response to surrender to Christ was due to his undiluted and unselfish love (Matthew 20:27-28; Philippians 2:8).

There are 5 things to remember when serving one another in marriage:

1. When you serve your mate, you are ultimately serving Christ. (Matthew 25:40)

When you demonstrate love by serving your mate, you are literally demonstrating your love for Jesus. You are worshipping him. He sees your sacrifice of love and you will not go unrewarded by him. Don't worry about what your mate does for you in return. You are doing it for Christ and it never goes unnoticed (which leads me to my next point).

2. When you serve each other, God himself will honor you. (John 12:26)

It's not unrealistic to have an expectation that your mate will show appreciation or even return your acts of loving service. However, even if it doesn't happen, we can always expect our

Heavenly Father to honor us. Honor from God is the best kind. Don't fret if your mate doesn't give back or respond adequately to your acts of service. Serving your mate will always reap a bountiful response from God (Luke 6:38).

3. Serve with a happy heart. (Ps 100:2)

There is a huge difference between just serving vs. having a servant's *heart*. How would my wife feel if I planned a date, bought her an expensive dress, made reservations at the most exclusive restaurant, picked her up in a limousine, hired a string quartet to play during dinner, and then looked in her eyes, reached for her hands across the table and said, *"Honey, I really didn't want to do this. I didn't have time and it was a real inconvenience, but I knew you wanted me to do it so I sucked it up and did it."* You know what would happen. Everything I did for her would be worth nothing because it wasn't from my heart. We should serve each other *gladly*. The attitude in which we serve goes a very long way. Resist the urge to grumble no matter the reasons (Philippians 2:14). When we complain about serving, whether it's voluntary or requested, it's like dumping *dirt* on what we do and it won't be received with joy. Nobody likes to feel like they're an obligation.

4. When you serve your mate you are also serving yourself. (Proverbs 11:25)

Sooner or later all that we do for each other will not be forgotten. We will see the fruit of our labor of love. Don't give up. Your marriage will reap the seeds of love that you have sown into it. Men: when you help your wife you are setting yourself up for a blessing. Remember; foreplay doesn't start in the bedroom, it starts in the kitchen; when you are doing the dishes. I once heard a woman facetiously say, *"I love to see my husband naked in the living room... pushing a vacuum."*

5. The way to the throne room is through the servant's quarters. (Psalms 84:10)

There is something about how God's presence, responds to loving, humble service. The scripture is clear that God gives us greater Grace when we humble ourselves and serve (James 4:6). Humility is no better displayed than when we serve. As we serve, God's Grace is poured out into our hearts and overflows into our marriage relationship. Grace is simply irresistible. Grace overflows from a serving heart, and it is that same Grace that will powerfully effect your marriage. When husbands and wives trust God and serve each other with no strings attached, he can move powerfully to strengthen the bonds of your marriage and break the chains of bondage in your marriage.

At the end of the day, when we serve one another, our motive shouldn't be to hear our spouse say, *"I appreciate you," or "I love you for that."* True, we like to hear those things from our mates and our love feels reaffirmed. However, we ultimately don't serve to get love. Rather, we serve because we are ALREADY loved (1 John 4:19). Christ's unconditional and unwavering love for us completely satisfies our deepest longing and overflows in abundant supply. Christ's love compels us to serve one another (2 Corinthians 5:14). We don't get our *love need* met by one another. Christ alone fully meets all our needs for love and acceptance. This truth empowers us to freely serve our mates with no strings attached.

We experience a greater measure of God's pleasure when we serve one another. Yet, we often hold back from fear that our serving will go unreciprocated and unappreciated. However, we must remember that experiencing God's pleasure is the ultimate reward. As we delight ourselves in him, it is his delight to meet our needs and fulfill our hearts desires (Psalms 37:4). Our greatest reward isn't receiving thanks from our mates, but rather hearing God say, "Well done." When we serve one another with this in mind, serving actually becomes our reward. We truly delight in seeing the other blessed. God delights when married couples demonstrate their love to one another in this way, and, in turn, he will respond favorably towards us.

"Well done my good and faithful servant."
(Matthew 25:23 NLT)

It is Christ's nature to love, and since we are partakers of his divine nature, we can wholeheartedly serve out of the essence of that love (2 Peter 1:4). When husbands and wives are motivated to serve one another out of a pure heart, they will in turn experience God's pleasure in their marriages. We will authentically serve one another in marriage in a much more gracious and loving manner when we operate in the Covenant of Grace.

Chapter 4

TELL THE LOVING TRUTH

At the beginning of our marriage, my wife and I made a hidden covenant of sorts, one in which we never discussed, but somehow we were in full agreement. For some reason or another over the years we've never really just come out and told one another we were gaining weight. Of course when Sherri and I were first married, being overweight wasn't an issue. We were in amazing shape, at the perfect weight, and so in love that it wouldn't have mattered anyway. However, as time went on we both began to change. I'm the one who began to put on some pounds. Of course my wife still looks as good as ever and that's the story I'm sticking with. Recent studies show that women who carry a little extra weight live considerably longer than the men who mention it. My wife has been very gracious with me, regarding my *areas of concern*. She still tells me I have big *guns* and great legs. She even points out from time to time that I have the best hands ever. Of course you can deduce what *areas* she's leaving out. To this day we frequently tell one another, *"You look great to me"* or *"I still think you're hot."* Over the years, Sherri and I have chosen to focus more on each other's good qualities. Are we in denial? No, most certainly not—well, maybe just a little. However, the point is that we have chosen to affirm the positive qualities in each other for the past 27 years of our marriage. We prefer to point out each other's striking features and not strike at the not-so-striking ones.

Marriages that focus on the good and affirm each other's strengths tend to be happier, more fulfilled, and grow deeper in the bond of love. Marriage begins to go *south* when we allow all the disappointments, hurts, and losses to affect our judgment, and thus, begin to more rigorously analyze one another. When we analyze, we eventually criticize. The thing that attracted us to one another now becomes the distraction. A law-based marriage is one that gradually hammers away at one another's inconsistencies. Ironically, when we try to *hammer* the nails of marriage in hopes to seal it, the same hammer eventually beats the marriage to pieces. Your spouse will never measure up to the standard of the Law outside of the Grace of God. The Law operates like a cruel task master that is never satisfied with even our best performance. Husbands and wives who operate in Grace choose not to point to one another's sins and shortcoming but only to the Christ in one another. In a Grace made marriage, couples choose to live on the side of affirmation, embracing all the curves, edges and perfect imperfections in one another. A Grace centered marriage focuses on the pure, admirable and lovely qualities in one another (Philippians 4:8). True, we will see areas of concern in our spouses that need to be pointed out along the way. We can't live in denial. I'm grateful when my wife tells me when I need a mint or to trim that one straggling nose hair. I don't typically relish in these honesties, but I'm thankful she doesn't let me venture into public with the potential of being embarrassed. Of course, the older my wife and I get the less we are able to see these things like we used to. Just the other day I told my wife we were going to have to buy one of those "old people" mirrors. You know the ones that have a regular reflection on one side but magnify 5X on the other side. Oh the things you miss when your eyes start to grow dim. On a deeper level, I also need my wife to lovingly and graciously make me aware when I am impolite, ill-mannered, aloof, rude, selfish, egotistical, etc. I don't want to cause harm or even permanently damage my relationships with others. However, the spirit by which I am made aware of these things can actually be detrimental in the marriage. If my wife regularly scolds me for these things it will have a negative result. The spirit of the Law is critical and demeaning in nature, while Grace effectively influences and positively shapes our behavior. Some couples believe that it is totally appropriate to point out all the *hard stuff* even if it comes across in a emotionally confrontational manner. It's, *"I love you, but I need to be plain."* However, much to their dismay, couples often discover that "telling it like it is" actually backfires. Somehow husbands and wives have used the following verse in Ephesians to justify bluntly telling each other the cold facts regardless of their approach.

"Instead, speaking the truth in love, we will grow to become in every respect the mature body of him who is the head, that is, Christ." (Ephesians 4:15 NIV)

To better interpret this verse, we must understand the times and context in which it was given. The Jewish legalists were continually pressuring young believers who were joyfully discovering their new found freedom in Christ, to continue conforming in accordance to strict religious adherence to the Law (i.e. do this, don't do that, eat that, don't eat that, wear this, don't wear that, measure up, comply here, etc.). Paul's response to the fervent legalistic rhetoric was for believers to be true to love; to speak only of what Christ had accomplished and the effects of his Grace in their lives. Paul's admonition was for early believers to avoid the harsh criticisms that many religious leaders were spewing. He further encouraged the believers to speak to each other with words of affirmation, love, and grace, reminding one another of all that Christ had accomplished. By this, they would continue to be built up into a mature body of believers that reflected the true image and radiant beauty of Christ. Young's Literal Translation renders Ephesians 4:15 like this…

"And, being true in love, we may increase to Him in all things, who is the head—the Christ" (Ephesians 4:15 YLT)

When husbands and wives are "true in love;" holding fast to speaking in a pure, lovely, and praiseworthy manner toward one another, it in turn fortifies and builds up the marriage into Christ like maturity. When couples focus on all that is lovely and admirable in one another, they actually will extract it from one another. Paul admonishes us to look for the best in each other and speak of it as often as we can.

"Finally, brothers and sisters, whatever is true, whatever is noble, whatever is right, whatever is pure, whatever is lovely, whatever is admirable--if anything is excellent or praiseworthy--think about such things." (Philippians 4:8 NIV)

According to New Covenant Grace, husbands and wives should endeavor to remove all condemning, critical words and harsh tones from their vocabulary and conversation and make a consistent effort to keep it out of the relationship altogether. When couples make it a practice to speak warmly, lovingly, kindly, tenderly, and affectionately, they in-turn preserve their admiration and loyalty to one another. That's what it means to be true to love (Ephesians 4:15) and how to truly stay IN love with one another.

"Let no corrupting talk come out of your mouths, but only such as is good for building up, as fits the occasion, that it may give Grace to those who hear." (Ephesians 4:29 ESV)

Corrupting talk is that which brings death, depression, discouragement, and sorrow to the mind and emotions. Have you ever heard the tone in someone's voice when someone says, *"I'm just going to tell it like it is."* The accompanying tone of their voice usually sounds harsh, judgmental, and vindictive. There is nothing gracious about it at all. Paul instructs us to be gracious with our words, not just say things graciously.

"Let your conversation be gracious and attractive so that you will have the right response for everyone." (Colossians 4:6 NLT)

There is no scripture that tells us to be brutal with our words. You don't have to be abrasive to be persuasive. In fact, the literal translation of *speak the truth in Love* actually means to *tell the loving truth.* The Holy Spirit doesn't point to our weaknesses; he helps us in our weakness. The Holy Spirit never tells us what's wrong with us; he tells us what's RIGHT about us. The Law reminds us of what we used to be, but Grace reminds us of who we ARE: beautiful, redeemed, accepted, holy, pure, righteous, and that we belong to Christ forever. The Holy Spirit defends us. He is our advocate and our defending attorney.

> **"But the Helper (Comforter, Advocate, Intercessor—Counselor, Strengthener, Standby), the Holy Spirit, whom the Father will send in My name [in My place, to represent Me and act on My behalf], He will teach you all things. And He will help you remember everything that I have told you."**
> **(John 14:26 AMP)**

When Satan accuses us of our failures and points out our weakness, we must listen to the words of truth of what Christ says about us. Jesus said "I am the truth." It's not what you did or how you failed. When we fail, the Holy Spirit doesn't point to our failure, he points to Jesus, the one who is our perfect righteousness. The Law obsesses about our failures but Grace points to the Christ in us. THAT'S the truth he speaks about us. The truth isn't that we failed but that Christ succeeded for us. Jesus says, *"I will never leave you, I love you, you are my own, you are my favorite, you are all mine, you are beautiful, you are redeemed, you are perfect in my eyes."* Likewise, this is the pattern of a Grace made marriage. We don't bring out the best by pointing to the worst in one another. When husbands and wives speak words of affirmation and point out the strengths in one another, they actually bring out the best in one another. This is the way Christ speaks to us.

"Christ's love makes the church whole. His words evoke her beauty. Everything he does and says is designed to bring the best out of her, dressing her in dazzling white silk, radiant with holiness." (Ephesians 5:25 AMP)

Did you see that? Christ's love makes us whole. His words evoke or summon our beauty. Likewise, your words evoke the beauty in your spouse. Every word we speak should shine the light on the beauty in one another. Our words have the ability to throw a black shroud over one another or either dress us in dazzling white silk. We should never demean one another regardless of the flaws. Christ's words never point to our flaws. Affirmation is the language of the Grace made marriage. There is never anything more embarrassing than to see a husband or wife rolling their eyes and taking cheap shots at each other, especially in public. God's Grace doesn't humiliate. His Grace is humble. Jesus does not berate us; He is elated with us. Couples should follow suit. Now I realize it is not possible in a marriage to be perfectly affirming 100% of the time. However, a Grace made marriage leans more fully in that direction. At any given day one person in the marriage is not going to be at their best emotionally, spiritually, mentally, physically, etc. When this is the case, the other should not point it out. Instead they should look for ways to give more Grace. In my early days of ministry my wife and I knew a young husband who was always bashing on his wife's inability to cook and to keep a clean house (as if it was just the wife's job to do that). His constant smugness and rudeness was more than I could take. He even regularly pointed out her flaws in our newly forming young couple's group. His wife would smile and look as if it didn't bother her, but her eyes told the true story. It deeply hurt. At one point I got so irritated that I was prepared to let him *have it*. However, the Holy Spirit gently told me not to say anything unless I could speak with him about it in a civilized and loving manner. After sincerely praying about it, I finally felt a peace to speak to him. I invited him to dinner at a local restaurant one evening. After dinner, I began to share with him that he should find the one thing that he liked about his wife's cooking and brag about it in public as much as he could. In fact, to my surprise he politely listened to all I had to say and was sincerely remorseful and apologetic. The very next week he began to tell his wife how great she fixed a certain dish and it did a lot for this young woman's confidence and it even brought some temporary reconciliation to their marriage. Now I can't tell you she became the next Julia Childs and that they had a perfect marriage. The point I'm making is that this one little affirmation did so much good in their marriage. When we point out the positive in our marriages it gives us something to live up to, a challenge if you will, to be the best we can be. No one can truly live up to their full potential when they're constantly being put down. Husbands and wives will never get better when all they hear about is their weaknesses. When we hear THE TRUTH about who we are in Christ and how much we mean to one another, it will actually cross over into the areas where we struggle and ultimately elevate us over our weaknesses. Grace breaks the mastery of all sin and bondage over us (Romans 6:14).

Did you know that the Law actually empowers us to sin more. Some translations even say that the Law gives strength for sin to continue. I like what the New Living Translation says,

"For sin is the sting that results in death, and the Law gives sin its power." (1 Corinthians 15:56 NLT)

The more you point at someone's failure you beat them down and actually cause them to fail more. The Law beats us down but Grace builds us up. The Law breaks us in pieces but Grace heals us and makes us whole. Satan's main weapon is accusation. Whenever we fail, the devil will surely remind us of it. He'll say things like, *"You failed," "You blew it," "You're no good."* However, the Holy Spirit does just the opposite. When we fail, he covers our weakness, defends our righteousness, confirms our holiness, and reminds us that we are totally pleasing to God because of Jesus' finished work in us. The Holy Spirit stands up for us and fights for us. When your spouse fails, you must ask the Holy Spirit in you to help you treat them in the same manner. Until then, you will never be satisfied in your spouse because they will always have opportunity to fail. We must see our spouses in the same way as God sees them. This is not to say that our mates will not have issues to overcome, and even regularly struggle with. Yet, just like you, God is working in your spouse to bring them closer to wholeness in the image of Christ. When husbands and wives cover one another with fervent prayer, unconditional love, abundant grace, and liberal amounts of mercy, patience and understanding, we can leave the results to God and trust that eventually we will see positive transformation in our spouses.

If we are to invite Grace into the marriage then we must cooperate with the Holy Spirit. We cannot act in opposition to how the Spirit operates in each other's lives. If he affirms, then we too must also be affirming. We take our lead from Him. What he says we should say. Therefore we must know how he speaks and what he speaks. He speaks gently in affirming, gracious tones. In the Old Testament God spoke to Moses from the MERCY seat (Numbers 7:89). The Holy Spirit always speaks to us from a place of mercy. Thus, we must speak mercifully to one another, reminding one another daily of who we are in Christ. Your spouse will become a reflection of the words you speak. If all they ever hear is criticism, they will certainly live up to it, or come down to it, as is the case.

Did you know that the words you speak to your spouse are like a mirror that creates an image of how they see themselves. If you speak favorably they will see themselves in a favorable light. If you speak demeaning of them... Well you get the picture. Often the reason our spouses fail to live up to their potential is because they eventually believe the negative words we say about them. According to James 1:23-25 when we look into the *mirror* of the Old Covenant, we see where we have failed to live up to it's standards. However, James goes on to point out that if we gaze intently into the mirror of the *perfect law of liberty* (Grace) the reflection will show that we are redeemed, holy, righteous, accepted, loved, adored, beautiful, radiant, perfect, and amazing in God's sight. As a result, we will become more effectual doers of the word of God because we see ourselves as redeemed. In effect, we become what we behold about ourselves. Likewise, our words are pictures we create of our spouses. The more they look into the pictures we paint of them, the more they will begin to believe what we say and ultimately become what we say about them. Are we *Law mirrors* or *Grace mirrors* for our mates? Do our words reflect the tender words of Christ to one another?

> **"Speak tenderly to Jerusalem. Tell her that her sad days are gone and her sins are pardoned." (Isaiah 40:2 TLB)**

If all I do is point out where my wife has failed, where she doesn't satisfy my expectations, and constantly poke at her flaws, I will not be able to speak into her life. Even more detrimental to our relationship, she may eventually ignore me all together. This happens all of the time in marriage. Couples eventually *tune* one another out, push each other away, and sabotage the potential for true intimacy. Spouses go to their *corners* and avoid connection altogether. However, if husbands and wives become *Grace mirrors* for one another with their words, reflecting affirmably of who they are in Christ, it will cause the marriage to be all it can be. We become what we behold.

> **"But we all, with unveiled face, beholding as in a mirror the glory of the Lord, are being transformed into the same image from glory to glory, just as from the Lord, the Spirit."**
> **(2 Corinthians 3:18 NASB)**

Paul says here that when we look into the mirror of God's Grace we actually behold the Glory of the Lord looking back at us. We are a spitting image of Christ because of all he has done in us. That's who we are and that's what we should see. When we see ourselves in the image of Christ (the glory of the Lord) we are transformed into that same image. When our words reflect what our mate truly looks like to God, they will be transformed into the same image, from glory to glory. They will eventually reflect the same qualities as His Spirit. Not only this but we are more attracted to one another when we affirm each other in Christ and confirm the work of his Grace in our marriages. Your words of Grace (speaking the loving truth) will have a profound effect in your relationship.

It is not only needful to speak words that build one another up in each other's presence, it is also a powerful relational principle in marriage to speak highly of one another when you are apart from one another. For instance, men, when you get together with the guys, don't use it as an opportunity to make snide remarks and even jokingly demean your wife, calling her a nag, boss, slave driver, etc. Ladies, when you spend time with other women, don't refer to your husbands in a negative light (i.e. dead beat, lazy, good-for-nothing, jerk, etc.). Husbands and wives, should defend one another. When you speak positively about your mate in the presence of others, it polishes your own image of them and creates a stronger bond even when you are not together. It will make the next time you see them all the more exciting. Speaking favorably about our mates in the presence of others increases our anticipation of seeing one another at a later time. One note of caution: If your marriage is struggling, and it is difficult for you to respond positively to the negative marriage banter and even spousal slander from others, try to remember the best things you can about your mate and speak of it. Refuse to participate in negative conversations about your marriage around those who are not trusted and godly friends. By all means don't open your heart and share the difficulties in your marriage with bitter and resentful people who are considering divorce or have divorced and have nothing good to say about marriage at all. Talk well of each other as often as you can. It will only help strengthen your marriage.

Husband… The words you speak about your wife are a mirror for her; a reflection of who she is to you. Wife… The words you speak about your husband is a mirror for him; a reflection of who he is to you. If you start speaking words that reflect the truth of who your spouse is in Christ, you will begin to see amazing things happen in your marriage.

Chapter 5

FORGIVING FORWARD

Grievances are like garbage. The longer they stay in the trash can, the more they pile up and eventually overflow. The smell and odor grow worse. Unforgiveness festers until it's presence overtakes everything and everyone it comes in contact with. In Alexander Pope's famous Essay On Criticism, he says, *"To err is human, to forgive divine."* Everyone sins, but we act most like God when we forgive. Husbands and wives are tempted to hold onto offenses. This is because sensitivity, vulnerability and transparency are intensified in the marriage relationship. There's no hiding and no covering up who you really are. Your personality is what everyone knows about you, while character is what your spouse knows about you. The longer you live together, the more will be revealed about you: the good, bad, and ugly. You won't be able to disguise your irritability, anger, irritation, insecurity, ungratefulness and all the things you work so hard to hide from the rest of the world. In the marriage relationship all is out in the open. Not only will you be unable to hide your issues, but those same issues will also greatly affect your spouse. Just like joy, happiness and elation are contagious in the marriage, so is irritation, anger, bitterness and selfishness. When your mate offends you, it's tempting to hold onto it without noticing until eventually you've harbored more offenses than you can count. These undetected offenses can even eventually contaminate your perception of the person you once fell in love with. Some feel they have reached their *limit* of offenses and contemplate ending their marriages. Unresolved offenses, are like knots in a string. Eventually, the string becomes so tangled it's hard to separate the first knot from the last one. If each grievance isn't dealt with as they occur, your relationship may wind up a tangled mess. So many marriages are tangled in offenses that it is difficult to remember exactly where they all originated from. That's why the scriptures are so explicit to treat each other kindly, tenderhearted, and forgiving one another just as God in Christ also has forgiven us.

> **"Be kind to one another, tender-hearted,**
> **forgiving each other, just as God**
> **in Christ also has forgiven you."**
> **(Ephesians 4:32 NASB)**

Kindness, tenderheartedness, and forgiveness are gifts of Grace from God in Christ. This is the foundation of a Grace centered relationship. We've been forever forgiven by God. In fact, forgiveness is not a one-time act by God in relation to each time I sin. No! Forgiveness is a gift I continue to receive for all my past, present and future sins.

> **"In him we HAVE redemption through his**
> **blood, THE FORGIVENESS OF SINS, in**
> **accordance with the riches of God's Grace."**
> **(Ephesians 1:7 NIV)**

As blood-bought believers, forgiveness isn't something we get; it's something we always have. It was a gift given to us upon our salvation and stays with us for the duration of our Christian lives. It is a permanent gift of God's Grace. Forgiveness is continually being extended toward us long before and long after we sin. It's perpetually proactive. When we sin, forgiveness is already going out to us. Through Grace, we have all the forgiveness we'll ever need. While hanging on the cross Jesus said, *"Father, forgive them for they know not what they do."* (Luke 23:34). Thus, demonstrating in his death something overwhelming and ever so glorious about forgiveness: God's forgiveness goes out before offenses come in. Have you ever been in a relationship when you asked forgiveness and the person put his hand out before you had a chance to speak and say, *"It's alright. I forgive you. We're good. You don't' even have to ask."* That's true forgiveness. It's proactive. It's already in motion, looking for someone or something to forgive. True forgiveness doesn't wait for you to ask, it just forgives. Forgiveness emanates from the Father's heart. He doesn't hold grudges. It's not in his nature. He doesn't pout in the corner until you come find him and then beg for forgiveness. Likewise, this is how couples should be with one another. Husband and wives cannot afford to hold onto the slightest grudge even for a second. *Forgiveness is the only option for the Grace made marriage.* Men are traditionally much better with forgiveness than women. They can have *words* and even "take their ball and go home" but then the next day come back and laugh about it. Men can argue, fight, and hash it out, but then forget it ever happened. Men can apologize to each other and that is usually sufficient to resolve conflict. However, women are much different. Women in general have to *feel* an apology. They are not normally convinced with mere words because their emotions typically run deeper. They have to be convinced you are sorry. It is even harder for most women to say they are sorry because they have to feel very sorry before they say it. This is why men typically have to apologize several times and prove their remorse before their wives unfold their arms and welcome their husbands in for the hug. This, of course, isn't true in all relationships. Some men have the same emotional complexity when it comes to apologies and forgiveness. However, emotional make-up is no excuse not to forgive. Granting forgiveness does not depend on behavioral temperament to be granted or the magnitude of the grievance. Some mistakenly feel they are guarding their hearts from reliving past bitterness. They'll say, *"I'll never allow myself to be hurt again,"* Nevertheless, they mentally and emotionally relive the past when they say it. Unforgiveness is like drinking poison and thinking it's killing the other person. It's ironic that so many couples are praying for open doors in their marriages, yet they persist in building walls of division, bitterness, and unforgiveness. Unforgiveness stays at work building the walls that keep hurt in and hope out. Every time you remember a grievance, you momentarily relive it, and by doing so, you add a another chain link to the fence of offense. If you don't intentionally come down from your fences, you will eventually fall into offenses.

Forgiving others is one of the ways we can truly guard our hearts from being hurt. To have a joy filled marriage, you have to love like you've never been hurt. I believe it is totally possible to have a *bitterless* marriage. How? By forgiving each other of everything, before it ever occurs and especially after it occurs. A marriage that forgives is truly a marriage that lives.

"A happy marriage is the union of two good Forgivers." ~ Ruth Bell Graham

Marriage is not about the ring you wear on your finger but the sign you wear on your heart — and the sign says, "I Forgive You." Offenses are impossible to avoid. As long as you are married, you will have to tack an invisible sign on your heart that says, "I Forgive You." Husbands and wives will have plenty of opportunities to be offended by each other which means the opportunities to forgive will never run sparse. Offenses + Apologies + Forgiveness = Marriage!

I'm going to share a secret with you... Your spouse is going to break more than one promise at one point or another... and so are you. Most husbands and wives break promises, big ones and small ones. God forbid that the biggest promise of all is broken and infidelity becomes an issue. This is always one of the toughest broken promises to walk through. However, when promises are broken, what will you do? Will you choose now to forgive, or have you placed limitations on what you will forgive and what you will not. Many marriages deeply struggle with severe issues of infidelity and broken trust. The greater the offense, the greater the opportunity for you to welcome the Holy Spirit to empower you to forgive. When you forgive, you allow the power of the Holy Spirit to work in your life. Letting grievances go isn't always easy. No one said it would be. However, one of the reasons the Holy Spirit was given was to help us forgive and overcome grievances. It's God's power working in us that enables us to forgive. *Although some offenses may not be forgotten, they can always be forgiven.* Scripture doesn't tell us to forget offenses. It only says to forgive them. Some offenses will come back to mind periodically, some even over the course of your marriage, and that is when you must choose to forgive again. When you are deeply hurt by the offenses of your mate, you have the chance to invite the Holy Spirit to manifest himself in your life. Be assured, the Holy Spirit never manifests as unforgiveness. When he comes, he comes to restore, revive, and rekindle the marriage relationship. The Holy Spirit will not help you hold onto a grudge. You must hand your hurts over to him if your are to heal. He is your helper. He does not want you to hold onto anything that will destroy you. When you choose not to forgive, you actually increase your potential for more depression and anguish. When the hurt is greater, the more opportunity you have to release the power of God to forgive.

Forgiveness is a gift of grace. Furthermore, it is a gift of grace that you not only give to your spouse, but a gift you give yourself. When you forgive your mate, you free them and also free yourself from the heavy burden of bitterness and resentment. Also, keep in mind that grace never makes demands even in the worst of situations; it just forgives. In fact, God extends more grace is in the worst of times. The Law condemns us at our best but grace forgives us at our worst. God's forgiveness is extended MORE when we LEAST deserve it. If forgiveness is to have the redeeming power it was meant to have in your marriage, you must allow it to operate in the same way that Christ freely gave it to you. Forgiveness brings bitterness to it's knees. When your mate hurts or offends you, don't punish yourself by allowing unforgiveness to linger. Give grace and forgive. Know that grace and forgiveness is far more powerful than any sin, hurt, heartbreak, failure, and any broken place in your marriage.

"...but where sin increased, Grace increased all the more..." (Romans 5:20 NIV)

One translation of this passage says, *"where sin abounds, Grace does much more abound."* There is no situation, drama, tragedy, failure, pain, sin, mistake, or mishap in marriage that exceeds the reach of God's Grace. The greatest stories of restored marriages I've ever heard came from marriages that chose not to give up and believe God for the impossible. Believing for a miracle in your marriage is not always easy, especially when infidelity is involved. God fully identifies with the infidelity issue. We have all sinned against him (Romans 3:23). We are all guilty of breaking his heart. We have all betrayed him. Yet, God proves his unconditional love, grace, and forgiveness. His selfless act of love is stronger than all our acts of infidelity combined. I don't know about you, but I am forever grateful for God's forgiveness. Where would any of us be if not for his mercy (Lamentations 3:22-23)? *God's forgiveness has taught me that our forgiveness in marriage must be stronger than our spouse's ability to apologize.* If our ability to forgive is based on the level of our mate's offense then we are not drawing deep enough from God's heart for the power to forgive. Sometimes in marriage the only thing you can do to survive is to forgive. There will be seasons in your marriage that you will find yourself dangling by a single strand of forgiveness. However, if we live our lives in eager anticipation to forgive one another, we will never be caught off guard. This is not to say that our spouses won't surprise us and even shock us sometimes with offenses that seem to come out of nowhere. This is because there is past brokenness in all of us and we carry these areas of brokenness into the marriage. Some more than others. Don't think that marriage fixes the brokenness in your spouse. In fact, marriage has the potential to multiply the brokenness because now it's brokenness x 2. That's what's interesting about the story of the prodigal son in Luke 15. The scripture says, "while he was a long way off" the father ran to him. Sometimes your mate might be a "long way off." That is all the more reason why you need to reach out to them in love and forgiveness. Forgiveness isn't tolerating, overlooking, ignoring, or shrugging off your mate's inconsistencies. Forgiveness is loving your mate in spite of their inconsistencies. The scriptures tell us that love covers a multitude of sins (1 Peter 4:8). When someone is wrong, we should respond rightly. When our mates are struggling (even deeply) with emotional issues, past grievances, and a long history of pain: love is the answer. When you marry someone, you not only tie the knot, but you get all their *knots* as well. I can't speak for my wife as she comes from a very strong, healthy and emotionally secure family. I on the other hand, come from a sordid history of family dysfunction, abuse, neglect, and childhood trauma. Of course, this was before my aunt and uncle rescued and adopted me in my early teens and lovingly brought me into their Christian family. However, even after I was adopted, I still had much to work through. During the first few years of our marriage, God gave my wife an exceptional amount of patience and understanding. She never stopped believing in me in spite of my dysfunctional behavior stemming from my early formative years prior to my adoption. Now, thanks to God's amazing Grace, I've been healed, set free, and the chains of my past have been completely broken. The point I'm making is sometimes in marriage one may have more baggage than the other. More than often, both in the marriage have significant emotional and psychological baggage to unpack. We are all *damaged goods* to some degree. Whatever the case, couples must realize that marriage is two people bringing baggage into the marriage. Grace provides a platform for couples to patiently sort through their emotional luggage together and by God's grace find love, mercy, forgiveness, restoration, and healing. When there's dysfunction x 2, that's when you need Grace x 3. Grace always supersedes and overcompensates for any issue no matter how difficult. Couples must give more than just temporary allowances of forgiveness. Allowances are granted when one has paid their fair share in the relationship. The problem with this is when the giving runs short allowances eventually run out. Allowances are typically given in response to the efforts of each individual. However, this is not how grace operates. Grace bestows forgiveness based on what Christ has done for you not what your mate does for you (or in some cases to you). Our capacity to forgive is in direct proportion to receiving Grace from God. When God is our source, we will never run out of forgiveness. When we depend on God's grace to help us forgive, we will always have an overflow for even the greatest offenses.

When the Father of the prodigal son saw his son a "long way off," he ran to him (Luke 15:11-32). He didn't even wait for his son to apologize. He ran full speed ahead and collapsed on him with forgiveness. Oh, that we would fall into one another's arms with forgiveness in our marriages. When your mate is a "long way off" is not the time to run away, it's the time to run into them. Instead of falling out with one anther, we need to lean into one another. It's not easy to do when you are hurt, but it's the only way to heal. Great marriages have learned to *lean in.*

Most marriages that are in crisis today are faced with the forgiveness dilemma. There are too many offenses, but seemingly not nearly enough forgiveness. A crisis in physics is when the velocity is too great for an object to make directional adjustment. For example, if someone is driving too fast and there's a sharp curve in the road just ahead, if he ignores the road signs and fails to apply the brakes in time, it may result in the car running off road. Likewise, prolonged offense and unforgiveness can keep a marriage in crisis making it difficult for couples to *make the turn*. However, the moment couples forgive each other they are able to reverse the effects of offense and effectively begin the process toward healing and restoration. So many couples wait to be healed so they can forgive; but forgiveness in marriage precedes healing in marriage.

One of the most inconceivable aspects of our forgiveness is that it cost Jesus everything but costs us nothing. He paid it all to forgive. The expectation from God is that since we have so freely received this forgiveness, then we should all the more liberally give it to one other (Matthew 10:8). Grace seems to make no sense at all. Law based relationships dictate that we give only in proportion to what we are given and no more. However, that's not how grace works. Grace says we don't deserve any good thing, but we can have it anyway. So many times in marriage we wait for our mate to earn our forgiveness by installments until the offense *debt* is paid. However, since we have freely received forgiveness from God, we have ample supply to give without ever running out. Sadly, couples run out of reasons to forgive each other all the time. However, under Grace we never run out of a supply of forgiveness for those reasons. When we draw from the well of Christ's forgiveness for ourselves and our spouses, we will never run dry. Remember, forgiveness with God doesn't stop after a undisclosed number of offenses. His love and Grace are infinite. God never holds us in contempt, and therefore, we should resist the temptation to hold our spouses in contempt. Don't wait for the apology. Beat your spouse to the punch and just forgive. Forgiveness makes the first move. When you live in this manner, it puts you on the advantage, because it is always to your benefit to forgive. So often we wait for the apology from our spouses before we forgive. However, real forgiveness refuses to be held captive by an apology. Your capacity to forgive shows that offense cannot hold you bondage. You are not under the power of an apology but under the power of Grace. Scripture tells us that the mercy and forgiveness we receive is in direct proportion to the mercy and forgiveness we give (Matthew 5:7; 6:14; 11:26). Therefore, we should live in a perpetual state of forgiveness. Living is forgiving and forgiving is living. Those marriages that are thriving and experiencing the most joy are those that understand that *forgiveness isn't an event; it's a way of life!* If you are preparing to get married or newly married, you should prepare yourself for the long haul to forgive. Your spouse is going to offend you. Jesus promised us that it would be impossible to avoid offenses (Luke 17:1). The level of those offenses is yet to be determined. However, there are no real guarantees that you will not be hurt, burned, disappointed, or even greatly disillusioned. The degree of offenses greatly vary according to circumstances and time. Life is unpredictable. I'm not saying you should live in fear for what the other will do. Love focuses on and believes in the best in one another (1 Corinthians 13:7). However, the way you prepare for the offenses that are going to come is not to harden you heart, but rather to maintain a tender heart that is always open and willing to forgive.

> **"Be kind to each other, tenderhearted,
> forgiving one another, just as God
> through Christ has forgiven you."
> (Ephesians 4:32 NLT)**

Being tenderhearted is often inconvenient and costly. So many grow calloused and closed off. However, when you are hurt is not the time to close the door to love, but to swing it wide open for love. This isn't always easy but it's always best. Don't allow your heart to become hard. It's better to stay tenderhearted and get hurt than to be hard hearted and stay hurt even longer. People think that hardening your heart protects you from hurt. Actually it keeps the hurt in. If you harden your heart, life gets harder. So, if your mate hurts you, you can fix them real good... You can forgive them (Proverbs 25:21-22).

To some cultures around the world, the word forgiveness isn't so common. One such culture is the Zuni Pueblo Tribe. Amongst the Zuni's there is no actual known word for forgiveness. As early as childhood the Zuni's become locked in silence for the rest of their lives because they do not know the language of forgiveness. Bitterness and begrudging actually are a normal way of life for the Zuni people.[9] Thus, is with many marriages. Couples stay locked-up in prideful silence. Resentment pushes the mute button. It literally puts a marriage on hold. However, when Grace is central, there will always be a constant exchange of forgiveness. It is the standard upon which couples can rely on. It is impossible for couples to move forward in the relationship until they forgive. The Greek word for forgiveness is *aphesis* which means dismiss, deliver, pardon, send away, let go, pardon, or release someone from an obligation or debt. Unforgiveness is like a prison, but forgiveness is the key that unlocks the door to encounter true freedom. Bitterness is like a poisonous root that prevents marriage from fully blooming. That's why the apostle Paul admonishes us, *"Be careful that no root of bitterness spring up in you."* (Hebrews 12:15). Forgiveness kills the root of bitterness before it has time to lodge in our hearts. Unforgiveness literally causes us to flounder, but forgiveness causes us to flourish. In fact, forgiveness is directly tied to prosperity in the marriage. Forgiveness positions your marriage for increase!

"Truly, I say to you, whoever says to this mountain, 'Be taken up and thrown into the sea,' and does not doubt in his heart, but believes that what he says will come to pass, it will be done for him. Therefore I tell you, whatever you ask in prayer, believe that you have received it, and it will be yours. And whenever you stand praying, forgive if you have anything against anyone."
(Mark 11:23-25 ESV)

"Give us each day our daily bread and forgive us our sins, for we ourselves forgive everyone who is indebted to us…" (Luke 11:3-4 ESV)

"And the Lord restored the fortunes of Job, when he had prayed for his friends. And the Lord gave Job twice as much as he had before." (Job 42:10 ESV)

Look closely at these three passages. Mark 11:23-25 says before we ask God for anything in prayer or believe for mountains to be moved, we must forgive if we have anything against anyone. Notice in Luke 11:3-4 how receiving even our daily provision is directly tied to forgiveness. In Job 42:10 God restored all of Job's lost fortunes, and then some, only AFTER he forgave his "friends" (which were actually his critics and haters). When we walk in a continuous flow of forgiveness, we will live the *and-then-some* life! If you are believing God for restoration, healing, increase, and next-level prosperity in your marriage, have you considered forgiving and praying for one another? God's will for your marriage is no less than to super-abound. When you choose to walk in forgiveness with each other you set your marriage up for increase, blessings, and fruitfulness in every area (emotional, physical, spiritual, financial, etc.).

Husbands and wives are often merciless with their demands, inflexible with their expectations, constant with their criticisms and silences. On many occasions couples silently keep score for the most ridiculous things, like the way they chew their food to the way their voice sounds when they're speaking on the phone or even to the type of presents they give each other. Yet, what most often brings couples together in the first place is a connection that transcends all of these petty little things.[2] Southern novelist Walker Percy once said in his book "Love in the Ruins," *"We love those who know the worst of us and don't turn their faces away."* A constant presence of forgiveness is the foundation for transformation in marriage.[2] When we are loved in our guilt and weakness we blossom. A marriage founded on forgiveness puts away the scorecards. No one is ever the "innocent one." Every marriage is the union of two selfish people, fighting for their rights, their way, and hell-bent to win. That's why when we apologize it feels like we are losing. We would rather keep tension in the relationship than surrender our rights.[2] The world tells us to stand up for ourselves, to stick to our guns, but Grace frees us to lay down our weapons, because everything we long for we already have in Christ.

A marriage founded on forgiveness, always has hope. There is always a way forward.[2]

One of the best pieces of advice my wife and I ever received regarding forgiveness was during our premarital counseling. Our pastor admonished us to never go to sleep with unresolved issues.

"Don't let the sun go down while you are still angry." (Ephesians 4:26 NLT)

This is probably the one most powerful pieces of wisdom and advice that Sherri and I have held onto. When issues arise that seek to divide us, we have committed to talking them out no matter how long it takes. Keep in mind, this passage doesn't necessarily mean to resolve every little detail of the issue before the sun comes up. However, we should do our best to work things out within a 24-hour period. That being said, my wife and I have chosen to take this passage literally. We refuse to go to sleep with resentment and bitterness in our hearts. We never let anger sleep. Anger is a monster. A monster may go to sleep, but he will still be a monster when he wakes up. Couples may choose to go to bed with issues of bitterness and unforgiveness, but those issues will still be there facing them the next morning with even greater resentment and anger. Let me tell you, Sherri and I have had our share of sleepless nights, heated discussions and all-out arguing into the wee hours of the dawn. Yet, there has always been a resolve to resolve; a commitment to pursue peace before the sun peeks its way through our window. It has been one of the best things we have ever done for our marriage. Plus, our make-up sessions have been some of the most heavenly times in our marriage. In other words, the better the make up, the better the make-out (if you know what I mean)!

After all I've learned about forgiveness in marriage, I believe that *to the extent you are able to forgive is as far as your marriage will go.* Holding onto offenses is a dead end road. Just because you are living under the same roof doesn't mean you are truly living. Forgiving is living. It is a part of God's design in marriage. Forgiveness indeed is the way to have a divine marriage!

> **"Make a clean break with all cutting,**
> **backbiting, profane talk. Be gentle**
> **with one another, sensitive. Forgive one**
> **another as quickly and thoroughly**
> **as God in Christ forgave you."**
> **(Ephesians 4:32 MSG)**

Chapter 6

THE DANCE OF GRACE

About five years ago, I had a spontaneous and creative impulse (more of a crazy notion actually) that my wife and I should take ballroom dancing lessons. It actually was a gift to my wife. I've always wanted to learn how to ballroom dance and thought it would be great fun for our marriage. Now if you know anything about me, I have always had great rhythm in music. I am a professional musician, vocalist and songwriter. However, when it comes to dancing, well let's just say all my coordination and rhythm go *out the window*. I have no gift in dance whatsoever. As long as I am standing in one spot, my body can sway fairly well. However, the moment you ask me to move my feet, disaster is imminent. My wife on the other hand, is just the opposite. She can't sing to save her life (she would wholeheartedly agree with me). However, in the area of dance, she has it down pat. When I told her that I had signed us up for ballroom dance, she was elated. So the evening finally came and we showed up for our first lesson. Our dance instructor was from Brazil. His name was Paulo, a suave and sophisticated gentleman who seemed eager to begin our sessions. So I put my dancing career in his hands. Interestingly, I don't believe it was a coincidence his name was PAULO. The Apostle PAUL has been referred to by many theologians as the Apostle of Grace. It took him nearly two-thirds of the New Testament to build an air-tight case for the Gospel (God has such a sense of humor).

During our dance lessons Paulo mostly teased me about my dance bravado, as I tripped and stepped all over Sherri's feet. Heck, I even tripped over air most of the time. However, I at least chalked-up significant husband *points* for clumsily doing my best to show her I loved her. Sherri told me later that I have talents elsewhere (that's how she lovingly tells me I'm not very good at something). I love how she always tries to focus on the positive in my life.

Sad to say, my dancing dreams only lasted for three short sessions, but this whole experience taught me so much about Grace in marriage. The following insights are actual statements that Paulo made during our lessons that translate so well into the marriage relationship.

1. You must wear the right shoes.

Heavy-heeled, pointed-toed cowboy boots should not be used for ballroom dancing. Dance partners risk getting their toes crushed and shins kicked in. In order to dance gracefully, your shoes must be soft and flexible, with just enough grip and slide. Custom fit shoes are the best. This is so true for marriage. You cannot *dance* gracefully in marriage if you are wearing the wrong shoes. Marriage is not a wrestling match; it's a dance. Ephesians 6:15 instructs us to wear the shoes of peace. Grace promotes peace. Several times in the New Testament Paul starts his letters with the greeting, *"Grace and peace be unto you."* To be graceful is to be peaceful. Couples should seek to maintain peace in their marriages.

"Live in harmony with one another. Do not be proud… If it is possible, as far as it depends on you, live at peace with everyone." (Romans 12:16-18 NIV)

Like a good pair of dancing shoes, couples must learn to be soft with each other in their responses (Proverbs 15:1). Each partner should be bending and giving, compromising and preferring the needs of the other above their own. We must be able to slide and move with one another's changing emotions. When dancers are too rigid, stiff, unbending, and unyielding, they may stumble and bring the dance to a halt. Fluidity, change, and flexibility are so important in the dance of Grace. Custom shoes are like a *custom made* relationship. Did you know your mate was custom made by God for you? Until you recognize this, you'll never move together in sync with your partner. Matthew 5:9 says, *"Blessed are the peace makers."* When couples purpose to create and maintain peace, it makes for a blessed union. We are called to be peacemakers not just peacekeepers. Continued and unresolved strife in marriage produces every evil result (James 3:16). Therefore, couples should proactively look for ways to be at peace with one another, not just wait until crisis moments arise to attempt reconciling. In the earlier years of our marriage, Sherri and I stood on somewhat opposite sides of the political spectrum. Thus, we decided that we would not discuss politics, especially around

Sherri's father. This decision was not based on fear but out of respect for one another's stance on the issues. Now-a-days we are more on the same page. There will be different seasons in your marriage that you will have to apply grace to prefer one another in a desire to keep peace. This is how you put on the shoes of peace. *Remember, the way you dance with one another will determine the way you sleep with one another.*

2. You have to see eye to eye.

During our dance lessons, Paulo said, *"You have to look into each other's eyes before you make the next move."* Seeing eye to eye is maintaining unity in the marriage. Scriptures indicate that unity is crucial to a successful marriage relationship.

"Can two people walk together without agreeing on the direction?" (Amos 3:3 NLT)

"If a house is divided against itself, that house cannot stand." (Mark 3:25 NIV)

Seasoned dance partners know that direct eye contact signals each other to the next move. It's instinctive. They've learned to read each other's eyes. Direct eye contact in dancing not only signals the next move but more importantly determines if the move will be successful. In marriage you must see eye to eye before moving ahead. Note that seeing eye to eye is not the same as agreeing. You can disagree and have different opinions. However, in order to effectively make good decisions for the marriage and family you must share the same core values. For instance, a husband might want to buy a red convertible sports car because he has always dreamed of speeding the interstate with the top down and the music blaring. The wife is in sharp disagreement over this because they have the constant responsibility to haul their three kids to school, dance, sports, and church. If couples do not share the same core values on the importance of family and practical matters, they will not be able to buy the right car for their family. What about in-laws? The wife may think it's not important to respect her parents. To this she may often speak rudely to her in-laws. However, if couples share the same core values of love for each other and honor for their parents, they will treat each other's parents with dignity even when their in-laws appear to be intrusively opinionated and overbearing. Seeing eye to eye is deeply sharing the same core values. In order to make decisions effectively and move forward you should agree on what is the best for the marriage and family above yourself. When couples have the same core values in areas of religion, family, finances, raising children, career, ministry, etc. it will help them instinctively process good decision making together. Real difficulties occur when you make decisions without seeing eye to eye in these areas. You may ask, what about the little things in marriage, like purchasing small items? What about your daily routine and the clothes your wear? Don't we get any freedom to just be ourselves? Do we have to believe and do the same things all the time? Absolutely not! It's important to maintain individuality in the relationship. After all, part of the reason your mate was attracted to you from the beginning was because of your uniqueness. That being said, I've just learned that it helps to talk through everything with your mate. My wife and I have a commitment not to keep secrets in our marriage and to be deeply and intimately honest with one another. Keeping secrets blinds you to the other person. When you are blinded you can't truly see eye to eye. Closing the door to honesty opens another door to deceitfulness. To do this, couples must feel safe enough to live out in the open in their relationship. When you see eye to eye in marriage it creates a place of true intimacy and helps keep strife at bay. When there is strife in a marriage, it invites every evil presence into the home (James 3:16). Just like you can foster the presence of God through unity, you can actually create a demonic environment through strife. Unity doesn't mean you will have the same tastes or like the same things. However, seeing eye to eye requires that you believe in the same core values, especially in the very important matters of life. This is why mutual compromise is often necessary in order to take steps in the right direction. Also, maintaining respect for one another is important when differing views are evident. Again, you don't have to always agree, even on the important issues. However, you should always respect each other, especially when expressing your opposing viewpoints.

3. A woman's steps are more complicated.

In dance, the man is the one that pauses to guide a woman through her complex steps. However, dancing requires the woman to do a greater percentage of the moving. Their dance steps are more complex, just as is their emotional and mental processing (generally speaking of course). In fact, scientific research suggests that women require more sleep than men because their brains actually work harder and operate at a much more multifaceted level throughout the day. This is much in part to the way a female multitasks.[10] Because of the complexity of their brains, it is normal for women, in certain situations to have a greater cycle of difficulty when processing their underlying apprehensions and concerns. This explains woman's periodic resistance to a man's quick decisions. Typically men are much more adventurous and spontaneous in nature. They are ready to march out and conquer the world.

The differences between men and women's brains are so vast it would take another book to adequately illustrate this point. For instance, men tend to compartmentalize things. According to Mark Gungor, comedian, speaker, and author of *Laugh Your Way to a Better Marriage*, men have little *boxes* for every kind of activity and situation.[13] They have a box for their car, a box for their kids, a box for their job, a box for their marriage, etc. When they talk with their wives they like to keep only one box open at a time. Meanwhile a woman's brain is more like one big, twisted, balled-up wire where everything is connected to everything. Their minds never stop working and sometimes they over emotionally process things. This often explains why women can seemingly pull an incident out of mid air and begin discussing it (often much to men's confusion and dismay). Every situation a woman experiences will ultimately lead to one or more other emotional experiences they have had. When women have an emotional experience, they remember the life event it was tied to. This explains why women remember more events because they are typically more emotionally responsive to those events. On the other hand, men tend to collect their emotions all in one *box*.[18] Of course, this is not necessarily true across the board, but is certainly accurate in many cases. This also explains why women's brains may have a hard time shutting down. Too many things are tied together because their emotional responses may be similar from one event to the next. Men on the other hand have one *box* in their brains that is filled with… You guessed it… Nothing! This is their favorite box. This may enlighten wives as to why their husbands can seemingly do something completely brain dead for hours. Many men like to fish or even play video games for hours because it basically involves doing nothing. Ladies, when your husband is lying on the couch watching football, you can assume they have retreated to their *nothing* box.[13] Of course, this sounds funny but actual studies conducted by the

National Academy of Sciences and The University of Pennsylvania Perelman School of Medicine further suggest that women's brains are wired for processing multiple items at once, while men's brains are more wired for processing one activity at time.[14] The findings from this research can give us some insight as to women's increased level of intelligence. Scriptures may support this. Note that women are addressed first in several passages in the Bible. For instance, Paul addresses the wives first in Ephesians 5. He tells them to submit to their husbands. Understand that it takes just as much strength, if not more at times, to submit than to lead. Peter also addresses the wives first (1 Peter 3:1). In Proverbs 21, the word *prudent* means intelligent. Contrary to popular belief, men are not just looking for brainless bodies. They innately and deeply long for someone intelligent to help them. That's why God created woman as his "divine help" (Greek: *ezer*). Also notice that Jesus, immediately after being resurrected, gives his first instructions to a woman. Maybe he knew she wouldn't forget what he told her. Come on men... Let's just admit that we often tend to put things in our *boxes* and forget about them, while our wives rarely forget anything. This could possibly explain when it comes to disagreements and disputes, women tend to brood over things longer while men typically let things go much more easily. All being said, men should learn to be patiently understanding of their wives and loving guide their wives as they attempt to complete their *steps*.

During our dance sessions, Paulo said, *"Dancing comes more natural for women."* I would be nothing without my wife. It is because of her strength that I have been able to do what God has called me to do. My wife has often talked me out of my fears and insecurities and encouraged my faith. Men need not be insecure with the strength of their wives. Some men underestimate the fortitude of women. Men, if you think women are the weaker sex, try pulling the blankets over on your side of the bed at night.

Men, I encourage you to take things slower with your wives. However, wives should also be willing to work through their fears in order not to miss the exciting things God has ahead. Husbands must patiently give their wives time to *spin* and fully complete their move. Is it any wonder why James 1:14 says, "Let patience have HER perfect work." Did you notice that patience is refereed to in the feminine form? This is because women typically display greater patience, often diverting their husbands from taking unnecessary risks. Many times wives can help save their husbands from disaster in their careers and callings. I am grateful my wife felt inclined at a few junctures in our marriage to say "no" to some things I felt God "calling" me to. Many times, I was simply unfulfilled and impatient rather than feeling an "urgency" from God. Thank God, I have chosen to wait on her so many times only to my advantage and blessing in our marriage.

4. Men usually take the lead.

Men, you have to put your big boy pants on now. You'll just have to accept that you are the leader. I didn't say dictator, but you are the chief facilitator of the family and home. Your wife is looking to you for wisdom and leadership. All this being said, regardless of how couples minds are wired differently, a wife needs to feel a sense of confidence in her husband as he guides her through her complicated *steps*. If a woman is uncertain about her husband or if she perceives that he doesn't understand her, she may not make the moves he is preparing to make. Men should seek the Lord in prayer and know the Word of God on matters. Why? Because his wife is looking to him to have direction in the marriage. Women should allow their husbands to lead them in the marriage. On the other hand, if a woman is to trust her husband, she needs to feel confident that he is seeking God and hearing from him for direction in the marriage. Men cannot simply assume that women should automatically feel comfortable letting them lead. Trust, integrity, character, morality, and experience all play an important role in men's lives as they lead their wives. Men, if you can't lead your greatest ally (your wife), how can you fight your greatest enemy (satan) together?

It is also important to point out that men don't necessarily need to make all the decisions or have the final say-so in every situation. Women have an amazing God-given intuition. It is not a myth or an old wives' tale. Women can literally *feel* their environment. Men are the "doers" but women are the "feelers." A woman's intuition serves as a *early warning system radar* – an innate sensitivity. They really know when things aren't right. Men, should be careful not to discredit their wives' instinct and perception. Be open to it. Listen to your wives and even be willing to defer to them for decisions when you are not sure what to do. Rely on their wisdom and insight into matters and be prepared to concede to them if needed. Women have a God-given sensitivity radar that helps gauge the directional course of the marriage. In fact, many times I deferred to my wife's wisdom because deep down I trusted in her intuitive perception. Husbands and wives should never let pride keep them from listening and submitting to one another. It's not a man or a woman *thing*. It's a marriage thing!

5. Maintain variety in your dance moves to keep it interesting.

As you progress in learning more about dancing, the steps get more complicated, but they also get much more interesting. It reminds me of the story of Henry and Priscilla, a very elderly couple who had decided to turn in for the night, the exact same time they did every night for the past 50 years. As they crawled into bed Henry began to gently rub his wife's arm up one side and down the other. He then proceeded to do the same to the other arm. Priscilla perked up and thought to herself, *"O my, Henry is feeling a little frisky tonight."* It had been so long for the both of them but she was glad he was at least showing some interest after all these years. Henry then rubbed the side of Priscilla's right leg and then on to the other leg.

As he began to stroke her left leg he immediately stopped. Priscilla wondered why Henry quit so abruptly just when things were getting interesting. She asked Henry, "Why did you get things started and then all of the sudden just stop. Henry replied, *"I was looking for the T.V. remote and finally found it."*

What's the moral of the story? *Keep things interesting in your marriage.* Keep your love alive. Jesus said in John 10:10 that he came to give life and give it more abundantly. This means every area of your marriage. Marriage is not an institution. Marriage is an adventure, and every exciting adventure has an element of the unexpected. Sometimes its easy to get stuck in a rut in marriage. To remedy this you can do simple things like change where you eat out, keep dating, go for long walks, play board games, turn off the T.V. and go for a drive. Even be proactive in making sex interesting. The Bible says that the marriage bed is undefiled (Hebrews 13:4). This means that *anything goes* in the confines of consensual sexual intimacy. Husbands and wives can *lift the covers off* of their sexual intimacy. Literally! Try different things as a couple and communicate your likes and dislikes about your sexual intimacy often. Men, don't be unsatisfied with your wife. Tell her what you like. Women, tell your men what you like. By the way, men should know that sex doesn't always start in the bedroom. It often starts in the kitchen. The way you treat each other by day is how you'll get *treated* at night. By all means, keep sexual intimacy in the context of Biblical monogamy and good moral practice. However, you are allowed to be creative and have fun in the bedroom. Get mirrors, change up the lighting, wear things that arouse your mate, play soft music, take your time, don't rush it. Although I recommend having sex as often as you can, know that you will go through seasons where it is less frequent. You don't have to have sex all the time for it to be great. Whether you have sex for seven days or seven times in one day, sexual intimacy can be phenomenal, if you commit to making it great together. A great book I recommend for this is *The Sexperiment – 7 Days To Lasting Intimacy With Your Spouse* by Ed and Lisa Young. I can see all the men running out now to buy this book. A little secret fellas... You can download it much faster on Kindle.

Your marriage can be born again or bored again. The choice is yours. Don't let Marriage get monotonous and predictable. Schedule a date night at least once or twice every month and plan a get-away every few months. Never stop dating. You don't have to spend a lot of money. Change the scenery, move the furniture around... Yes men... Literally! Help your wife move the furniture around. Keep your marriage interesting. I don't think I need to give a lot of instruction or a manual illustration. That would require a different marriage course.

6. Dancing should be fun and romantic.

Romance and fun are the spice of marriage. They are the visible signs that the flames of love are burning in your relationship. No matter how long you've been married, every couple still needs romance (especially on important dates). Some religious people have a sour look on their face all the time. But Christianity should be full of joy. Marriage shouldn't be thought of as all "hard work." I want to abolish that concept. A Godly marriage is made by Grace, not hard work. The Law promotes work and much self effort to keep things afloat while Grace promotes Christ's work. Romance shouldn't be thought of as hard work, but a joyful effort to reinforce your true devotion for one another. Romance fuels the marriage. Things like holding hands, saying sweet nothings, flirting, tender touches, exchanging glances in large crowds, etc. These amorous gestures are like kindling in a fireplace. My wife and I love going out and spending time together whenever we get the chance. However, some couples don't go out anymore at all. Too many marriages have settled. If you don't date in marriage, your marriage might have an expiration date. Don't let that happen. Keep romance alive. Get out of the rut-hut and date often!

7. You have to commit for the long term.

Great dancers don't become that way overnight. Likewise, great marriages take a lifetime to make. Once a man was asked if he had a happy marriage. He replied, "I'll let you know in 50 years." Don't base your marriage experience on one bad moment. Marriage is for life. If your marriage is in a difficult *spot*, it doesn't mean your marriage is bad; it just means you're married. So many couples are ready to end it when tough times come. *Don't size-up your marriage based on the season of your marriage. Resist the urge to make a permanent decision in a temporary circumstance.* In other words, you and your spouse are in it for the long haul. Studies consistently suggest that the longer couples stay married, they will continually become more fulfilled and happier than they've ever been. In his book, *The Meaning of Marriage*, Dr. Timothy Keller' states...

> *"Studies demonstrate that two-thirds of statistically unhappy marriages will become happy within an average of five years if couples stay married and do not get divorced... Much of the research evidence suggests that... most people who are not happy in their marriage but do not get divorced will eventually become happy."*[4]

8. It's no fun to dance alone.

Sometimes inexperienced dancers are tempted to steal the show and outshine their partner. This is because they feel they have the dance moves down pat and by moving forward too quickly, end up looking like they are dancing alone. There's no such thing as solo ballroom dancing. It was made for two people. Marriage is about two people doing life together, learning together, growing together, walking hand in hand. Husbands and wives are simply better when they are together.

"Two are better than one, because they have a good return for their labor: If either of them falls down, one can help the other up. But

**pity anyone who falls and has no one to help
them up. Also, if two lie down together, they
will keep warm. But how can one keep warm
alone? Though one may be overpowered, two
can defend themselves. A cord of three
strands is not quickly broken."
(Ecclesiastes 4:9-12 NIV)**

In Genesis 2:18 God himself said, "It is not
good for man to be alone." In all that God
created, he ended each day by saying, *"It is
good."* But when he created man he said, *"It is
NOT good,"* So, he created a helper suitable for
him. We need each other to become all God
wants us to be. You can't get where God wants
you to be alone, so he gave you the perfect
companion to help make it possible (1
Corinthians 7:14). Part of the purpose of
marriage is to help reveal areas in our lives that
need to be sanctified, and marriage, like no
other thing, can be mightily used by the Holy
Spirit to do what he is exceedingly efficient at—
Sanctifying you! The end purpose of marriage is
to bless you AND to build you. Where did any
of us get the idea that we were perfect going
into marriage. The truth is, marriage helps us
discover the person we really are and better yet,
helps us discover the person we can be.

Selfishness is not a welcome trait in marriage: when one does more taking than giving. It is not fair if one person in the marriage is progressing in every area of their life, while the other is struggling just to keep up. One is getting all the extra time to pray, read the Bible, and immerse themselves in hobbies and other extra curricular activities that improve their overall quality of life; while the other spends all their available time working, taking care of the house, caring for the children and all the other responsibilities that come along with life and marriage. Couples should give appropriate concession to one another for personal development including such things as continued education, fun hobbies, friendships, spiritual development, physical exercise, etc. A husband and wife will benefit not only as individuals, but even more so as a couple when they both invest in and allow adequate time for each other to develop into more well-rounded people.

9. Dancing takes an incredible amount of grace.

During our dance sessions, Paulo reached for my forearm and said, *"Tony, I'm trying to position you for power. Grace is where you get your power. Dancing takes an incredible amount of Grace."* To have a long and fulfilling marriage, you need an incredible amount of Grace. God doesn't give us power over our mates, he gives us power for our mates, to serve, guide, love, lead, and hold. The power of Grace is gentle and peaceable. In dancing, you gently hold on to each other and gracefully move together in one single harmonious movement.

Humility is the posture of a successful marriage, and Grace is the position. When dancers approach each other, they take their stance and are poised to begin. Humility is how couples get poised for marriage. When you are postured correctly, you will execute the dance steps properly. Humility will attract the Grace of God in your marriage (James 4:6). There will be seasons where your marriage feels out of sync. However, if Grace truly abounds in the relationship, it will help you *dance* through the difficult times (Romans 5:20). Through an abundance of Grace, your marriage will not only survive, it can thrive through anything life brings.

"...much more will those who receive the abundance of Grace and the free gift of righteousness reign in life through the one man Jesus Christ." (Romans 5:17 ESV)

During our final lesson, Paulo told me that good dance partners don't dance flatfooted. He also told me I danced like a brute. He said, *"Tony, this isn't clogging; it's ballroom dancing! To be a great dancer, you have to be light on your feet."* To possess the Grace to dance, couples have to stay on their toes. You need to be ready for anything life will throw at your marriage. Don't be surprised when days seem hard and nights seem scary. Through the good times and bad times, keep dancing! Don't be flat footed, demanding, hard, and rigid in your relationship. Lighten up. Enjoy the days you have together. Life is too short to stay on opposites sides of the wall. You have to come together to dance. Dancing in marriage is all about giving each other liberal and unlimited amounts of Grace. I have always felt that I could conquer the world with one hand if my wife was holding my other hand. That's what marriage is. It's knowing you can conquer the world together. Couples who lean on the Grace of God can make it through all of life's challenges and changing seasons TOGETHER! So take each other by the hand, hold on tight, and gently step out onto the floor of life… and whatever you do, don't let go… and then… Just dance.

Chapter 7

AVOW AND ALLOW

Once I came across some funny advice about marriage from kids. I've had these in my files for a very long time, I can't remember where I got them, but all I can say is, "You're welcome!" Several children between the ages of 6-10 years old were asked their opinions on marriage. Brace yourself for their answers.

How do you decide who to marry?

"You got to find somebody who likes the same stuff. If you like sports, she should like it that you like sports, and she should keep the chips and dip coming." ~ *Alan, age 10*

What is the right age to get married?

"No age is good to get married at. You got to be a fool to get married." ~ Freddie, age 6

What do you think your mom and dad have in common?

"They both don't want any more kids." ~ Lori, age 8

What do most people do on a date?

"On the first date, they just tell each other lies, and that usually gets them interested enough to go for a second date."
~ Martin, age 10

What would you do on a first date that was turning sour?

"I'd run home and play dead. The next day I would call all the newspapers and make sure they wrote about me in all the dead columns." ~ Craig, age 9

When is it okay to kiss someone?

"When they're rich." ~ Pam, age 7

Is it better to be single or married?

"It's better for girls to be single but not for boys. Boys need someone to clean up after them." ~ Anita, age 9

How would the world be different if people didn't get married?

"There sure would be a lot of kids to explain, wouldn't there?" ~ Kelvin, age 8

How would you make a marriage work?

"Tell your wife that she looks pretty even if she looks like a truck." ~ Ricky, age 10

These are funny for sure. Yet, how often do we carry misconceptions of marriage from childhood into marriage. A woman may think that her husband should be Prince Charming and refuses to believe it any other way. She imagines living life in Cinderella's castle. On the other hand, a boy might dream of being Superman rescuing Lois Lane. These dreams are real, yet life turns out nothing like them. We often create fantasizes and then are sorely disappointed when marriage doesn't pan out like them. Sandcastles! So often we develop philosophies and ideals of marriage that aren't based on truth, and often aren't even founded on common sense.

One of the biggest misconceptions is that the promises we make in marriage are full proof. I can't speak for my wife, but I've certainly broken my share of promises in our marriage, some even significant ones. Isn't it interesting however, that we allow certain broken promises to slide and avoid discussions all together about them. We judge these things by the severity of the broken promise. For instance, some wives are typically good to over look unfinished "honey-do" projects in the house that their husbands have left undone, until one day they notice the jobs haven't been completed for six months and then explode.

Some men let their wives slide when a bill is unpaid, that is until they get a notice in the mail that the water is going to get cut off unless the past due balance is accounted for. We seem to leave certain things unaddressed only until we've had enough. It is tempting for couples to irrationally overreact at the most unpredictable times, catching one another totally off guard.

Couples must guard against wasting precious emotional energy on the insignificant issues in order to maintain capacity to handle the really important issues as they arise. Often couples make mountains out of molehills, but then when the real important matters present themselves they have little presence of mind left to handle them. There will be significant issues in marriage that couples cannot ignore or live in denial about such as: infidelity, finances, substance abuse, spousal or child abuse, etc. The serious pressures must be dealt with head on (with your head on). However, couples often allow themselves to get so exasperated over small things, that when the serious issues arise, they cannot appropriately process them. All being said, if you made a vow for marriage, then you must allow in marriage! What does this mean? It means that when couples make a vow in marriage they must, by

God's grace, allow each other as much time as it takes to redeem their actions. This is not saying that anything goes. Not at all! However, couples must understand that Grace has no strings or ultimatums. Strings tie couples down and hold them back from soaring. Grace releases a marriage to be all it can be. Many couples insist on creating airtight systems of accountability that have the potential to suffocate the marriage. It's do this or I will incessantly snub you or shut you out. Once it's done, then we're on good ground. This is the concept of earning allowances. As kids, we receive allowances through completed chores and fulfilled responsibilities. However, Grace gives allowances without earning because Grace is a gift undeserved or unearned. Understand that Grace is not opposed to effort, However, it is opposed to earning. I don't earn love from my wife because of what I do for her. I SHOW her love by what I do for her.

The following seven allowances have helped my wife and I more firmly avow our promises to one another while at the same time help us allow for room to breathe, and grow in our marriage. As you read through these points, openly discuss them with your spouse, and list a few of your own that have helped you in your marriage.

1. Allow for a lifetime of mistakes.

Being married for a lifetime makes for a lifetime of successes and failures. You can't have one without the other. The first way to approach your mate's mistakes is to remember that you also make mistakes. No one is immune to them. If at all possible, try not to resort to making accusations. Don't operate in the spirit of the accuser (Revelation 12:9-11). Rather operate in the spirit of the Forgiver (Colossians 3:13). It's easy to play the blame game especially when your partner is obviously at fault. However, a law based relationship expects perfection and is intolerant to failure. A Grace based relationship promotes an atmosphere of freedom and allows for mistakes. This in turn empowers each partner in the relationship to better rebound from failure. When we operate in Grace, we realize our mates are never perfect outside of Christ's redemptive work in their lives. By Grace, I understand my wife is my greatest ally. Rather than pull back when she is weak, I should all the more be drawn to her, just as Christ is drawn to my weaknesses.

"My grace is sufficient for you, for my power is made perfect in weakness."
(1 Corinthians 12:9 NIV)

When your spouse fails, your condemnation and demands for perfection produce nothing. Our expectation should be of the CHRIST in one another. We must see one another in Christ, just like God sees us. By this, we affirm our spouses of who they ARE and not what they've DONE.

2. Avoid pushing your agenda.

Several years ago Samsonite made a commercial to prove the strength and durability of their luggage. They tossed a locked suitcase into a gorilla cage and let him pound, stomp, slam, and claw to pry it open. Try as he may, he was unsuccessful, further proving that Samsonite could take the punishment. Many men are like this gorilla: extremely competitive and determined to prove their point at all costs. Husbands often resort to pressuring their wives to submit to their convictions. Conversely, I've also discovered that women can be a lot like skunks. If you back them into the corner for too long, they will eventually spray you. Skunk beats ape! Once my wife and I were in an *intense conversation* and I was attempting to push my scriptural revelations about Grace on her. Mind you, I wasn't being so gracious. In fact, I was being quite overbearing. At a heated point in our *debate*, she paused and lovingly said, *"Tony,*

Grace is a verb!" Instead of lashing out and fighting back, she took the alternative. She didn't accuse me of being a know-it-all or Bible snob. She responded in love. Her gentle response disarmed my delusions of superiority. No matter how strong and founded your opinions may be, you will not always be able to convince your spouse of the same. Whenever you are so sure about something and feel your mate is wrong, sometimes it helps to honestly ask God, "Am I as right as I think I am?" Be careful not to ask yourself this question as you often will tell yourself what you want to hear. That's why you should ask for GOD'S unbiased answer. Once you have asked, lay down your pride and wait for him to speak. Always remember, God doesn't answer prideful prayers. Let me give you some great marriage advice; Whenever you're wrong admit it; whenever you're right, remain silent!

3. Abolish all guilt.

Don't condemn one another, EVER! There is no condemnation for those who are in Christ Jesus (Romans 8:1). Your spouse should never have a reason to feel guilty in your presence. Completely and immediately forgive one another with no strings attached and forget their offense forever.

Oh the joy and love I feel when my wife forgives me. It's glorious! When we abolish all reason for one another to feel guilty, it fosters a climate of love in the marriage. Once again, we are to forgive one another before an offense is even committed (Matthew 18:12; Luke 23:34). True intimacy is born out of a deep confidence that you are accepted no matter what happens. Do not use your mate's offense for leverage. Use their offenses as an opportunity to love. This takes humility, but when we respond in this way we mature in the love of Christ.

When we open up our hearts to love instead of lash out, we grow in the Grace of God each time. When we give the gift of Grace, it actually gives back to us. When we abolish guilt, it serves to conquer the work of sin in the other person. When we build a pavilion of love over our spouses, we bring them under the canopy of Grace and actually release an atmosphere in our homes where sin continually loses is power (Romans 6:14). Abolishing all opportunity for guilt is a one of the most powerful forces that has kept our marriage unbreakable for 27-years. If you apply this same principle in your marriage, I am hopeful that you will experience greater joy and freedom in your marriage. Grace never fails!

4. Accept the differences.

Don't just tolerate one another. Celebrate one another, even the differences. People go where they are celebrated, and more importantly, stay where they are celebrated. This is a tried and true relational principle in life. Remember, if you don't celebrate your spouse, *someone* may be waiting in the wings to take the job for you. Celebration directs our senses and ambitions. God never evaluates us based on our performance. He delights in us period! We are clothed in the righteousness of Christ. Toleration and evaluation drive us away from each other in marriage. We can literally feel the tension in the room. Truth is, we all love to be celebrated. If we are celebrated more outside the marriage than we are inside the marriage, then we will be drawn away from the marriage. However, when we know that we are more affirmed in the marriage than anywhere else, we will be convinced where home is. We should not just appreciate each other's uniqueness, but also cherish and value it in each other. Take a moment and speak this scripture over your spouse further affirming them in God's grace. Put your spouse's name in the blank as you say it out loud.

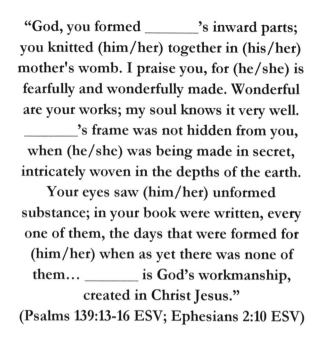

"God, you formed _____'s inward parts; you knitted (him/her) together in (his/her) mother's womb. I praise you, for (he/she) is fearfully and wonderfully made. Wonderful are your works; my soul knows it very well. _____'s frame was not hidden from you, when (he/she) was being made in secret, intricately woven in the depths of the earth. Your eyes saw (him/her) unformed substance; in your book were written, every one of them, the days that were formed for (him/her) when as yet there was none of them... _____ is God's workmanship, created in Christ Jesus." (Psalms 139:13-16 ESV; Ephesians 2:10 ESV)

If you see your spouse through the lens of Grace, you will discover that they bear a fascinating and striking resemblance to Jesus. Don't allow what once attracted you to one another to detract you from one another.

5. Acknowledge the process of change.

The other day my wife looked over at me and told me that I still had the "big guns" (meaning that my biceps were still large and in charge). At this, my 14 year old daughter looked up and said, *"I love it when old people flirt."* Truth is, both of you are going to change as the years roll on in marriage (physically, mentally, emotionally, etc.) Sometimes these changes will catch you by surprise. The person you used to be will not be the person you will become. Not all of the changes will be negative, but life brings change and you can choose to enter it with a negative attitude or enter it with grand optimism. Change comes to all. Our bodies change, our memory fails, our emotions fluctuate, our perspectives shift, etc. Not all changes are bad. People also mature, succeed in their careers, become more compassionate, disciplined, determined, etc. No matter life's changes or stages, love always focuses on the beauty in one another (1 Peter 4:8). Today my wife is much wiser, stronger, beautiful, insightful and mature than she has ever been. *It is entirely possible for your marriage to become sweeter as the years roll on when you determine to focus on the admirable qualities in one another.* You don't have to always understand the changes your mate is going through, but you can always love them regardless.[16]

Not only does change come in the physical and emotional, but also in the spiritual. Know that God is changing your spouse for the better. However, remember that transition always precedes transformation, and transition is often a messy process. When God works in our lives the metamorphosis is not always appealing at first. Earlier in this book, I mentioned that when we become older we take on new interests, new aspirations, new adventures, new revelations, and deeper insights to life and our individual callings. Many of these are initiated by God and must be allowed to unfold in God's timing. In Grace, we can lovingly and patiently embrace growth in our mates. At all times and seasons in the marriage, no matter how long you've been married, your mate will always be a work in progress (just like you). Although it might not look like it, your mate is being transformed into something more beautiful than when you first met them.

"And we all, with unveiled face, beholding the glory of the Lord, are being transformed into the same image from one degree of glory to another. For this comes from the Lord who is the Spirit." (2 Corinthians 3:18 ESV)

We must trust the Grace of God to have its perfect work in our marriages. You are not the Holy Spirit. Stop trying to control your spouse in attempts to slow down or stop the transformation process. For instance, if you tear open a cocoon and pull out the caterpillar to inspect it before it completes it's metamorphosis, you'll ultimately destroy the butterfly. Control is a symptom of fear not of trust. We fear our spouses getting out of the boundaries we have created for them so we attempt to regulate them. When you try to *adjust* your mates, it actually has the opposite effect. Stop trying to interrupt the work of God in your spouse's life. You'll only hinder the process and frustrate yourself (Galatians 2:21). Allow God's grace to do it's full work in it's full time. Grace is always patient. Therefore, we should be patient with one another during the process of change. The best way to support your mate is with humility, not with a hammer.

6. Avow your steadfast love regularly.

Repeated marriage counsel highly asserts that married couples should date regularly. *Remember, you are girl friend and boy friend before you are husband and wife or parents.* Truth is, if there were more courting in marriage, there would be fewer marriages in court. When you date often, you affirm your steadfast love. I like to think of dating as a regular mini honeymoon. Coming together often for fun, emotional intimacy and physical connection does wonders for your relationship. Good dating practice involves the following four things (D.A.T.E.).

D = Devotion: In order for dating to be effective, each person should be wholeheartedly devoted to it. One shouldn't be more enthusiastic about it than the other. Each person in the marriage has to be equally committed to make a regular dating relationship happen. Being committed to the dating relationship shows that you are devoted to each other. Remember, the marriage relationship is the most important relationship in the home; even more important than your relationship with your kids. Your children will eventually leave the home, but you and your mate are together forever. The marriage will last long after the kids are gone. If you always put your kids first, when they leave the home, all you have given your life to will have vanished. Many married couples find themselves not knowing the other person after the kids are grown and move out because they gave all their devotion to them.

A = Affirmation: Dating should always give attention to the other person. We should be more about the interests of our spouses first.

"...Rather, in humility value others above yourselves, not looking to your own interests but each of you to the interests of the others.

**In your relationships with one another, have
the same mindset as Christ Jesus..."
(Philippians 2:3-5 NIV)**

Take turns going out to places and involving
yourself in hobbies and interests the other person
enjoys (i.e. movies, shopping, restaurants, parks,
museums, antiquing, hiking, camping, etc). When
we apply this concept in marriage, the entire date
will revolve around the other person. Both will be
100% giving and 100% receiving.

T = Time: Time reflects priority. What you give
your time to shows your priorities. If the marriage
dating relationship is non existent, it could reflect
that the marriage is truly not the priority.
Therefore, dating shouldn't be ignored or rushed.
Plan to give ample time to your marriage dating
relationship. The rewards are ever unfolding.
Through regular dating you create affectionate
memories you and your spouse can refer back to
when times get tough. For instance, when there is
tension in the marriage and emotions feel stale,
you can think back on the special times you
shared. Regular dating helps to reignite the love
and romance in your marriage. I often go back to
times in my dating years when my wife and I first
met that stimulate and warm the embers of my
heart. When you date often, it's like throwing

kindling in the fire. The more you date, the more memories you make that keep the flames of passion alive.

E = Engage: When you date your mate, shut off all outside distractions. Put the mobile phones away. Look into each other's eyes, listen, talk, share, hold hands, touch, kiss, smile, look interested, be there, be present in the moment. God always listens intently to our prayers and gives full attention to us when we come to him.

> **"But God did listen! He paid attention to my prayer. Praise God, who did not ignore my prayer or withdraw his unfailing love from me." (Psalms 66:19-20 NLT)**

When we come to God, we desire that He attentively lean into us and listen to our prayers. We would be deeply hurt and even devastated if he turned away and ignored us (Psalms 27:9). Of course, we know God never turns his face away from us and so we should display the same Grace in our dating relationship and be totally *there* for one another other. Give your whole self to your spouse when you are together. Life is short. Savor every moment with the one God gave you.

7. Anticipate the best.

Finally, don't dread the worst in one another. See your mate as the righteousness of God in Christ (2 Corinthians 5:21). In other words, they are as righteous as God is. According to legalism, this is not the case. However, according to Grace, that's exactly the way God sees us: perfect in Christ's perfection. Therefore we need to use this type of language when we talk TO and ABOUT one another. When we speak of the imperfections in one another, we are no longer looking at each other through the eyes of Grace. We should use words that build one another up. Speaking faith over one another is how Grace operates. We are saved by Grace through faith (Ephesians 2:7-9). Therefore, our faith in one another will preserve and save the marriage. Just see what Grace-talk will produce in your marriage. Instead of saying, "We're just not what we used to be," may I suggest saying, "We are better than ever." Instead of, "I wish you were more like this person or that person." Say things like, "I love this about you…" or "I love that you are…" Instead of jabbing with, "You didn't used to be that way: critical, mean, hateful, unloving, inattentive, etc.," say, "You are becoming all God desires for you." Sometimes your mate is going through a very difficult time in their lives. This is not the time to pull away with your words and attitude. Life comes down on us all. *The best is yet to come* should be the theme of our marriages.

> **"For I know the plans *and* thoughts that I have for you,' says the Lord, 'plans for peace *and* well-being and not for disaster to give you a future and a hope."**
> **(Jeremiah 29:11 AMP)**

Sometimes in marriage, it may feel like you're drowning under an ocean of doubt, second guessing, and regret. That's when you need to rise above "see level" into the faith realm where you can see what God sees. It's normal to lose sight of God's promises for your marriage. This is why you must remember that God believes the best about your spouse. Never say anything different about them than God would say about them. Keep believing in your mate and more importantly believe in the work that God is doing in them even when you don't see it. After all, we are to walk by faith and not by sight. (2 Corinthians 5:7). Rest assured that all things are working together for the good for your marriage (Romans 8:28). That's a promise you can always count on.

Chapter 8

LET'S TALK INCOMPATIBILITY

Many marriages get stuck in the quandary of perceived incompatibility. Everyday couples discover they are not as compatible as they thought they were when they first met. When couples begin to realize they are more different than alike, they are tempted to think they've married the wrong person. They buy into the lie that because they have several areas of incompatibility they are no longer compatible as a couple. The future looks bleak. Let's be honest. How many marriages are truly compatible or have a majority of things in common? From the beginning of time, men and women have never been truly compatible. It doesn't take a dating website to figure this out. Speaking of dating websites, today millions of singles are turning to dating websites to find the perfect match: someone who is completely compatible with them. The fear of incompatibility in relationships drives this phenomenon. Many of these dating websites claim to have the marriage problem solved. They promise to help you manage the "issues" before they arise. Just fill out the 300 question survey and submit the 40 dimensions of compatibility form and we'll match you with someone who is "perfectly" compatible with you. The claims are they'll make marriage controllable, and by sifting through the endless questions, embellished bios, and photo-shopped profile pictures you'll find just the right one (out of the 7 billion people on the planet). *"Just enter our laboratory,"* they say, *"and we'll fix the problems before they happen."*

Of course I'm exaggerating. However, the point I'm making is compatibility tests will not eliminate the problems that are going to arise in marriage. No matter what marriage website you use to find a "match," sooner or later you are going to wonder if they are the same person you met in the first place. You may hope to maintain the illusion that you are in control of the parameters of the relationship. Furthermore, you may think you've figured out all there is to know about the other person before you marry them. However, no matter how much you think you may know about one another, the truth is, they are going to change. When people first meet and begin to fall in love, they easily look past all the differences and areas of possible incompatibility because they don't want to *spoil* or *spook* the relationship. However, not too long after the knot is tied, some couples act surprised that they are so different after all. Folks, men and women are from totally different galaxies. It's black and white, Sonny and Cher, chocolate and vanilla, hot and cold. Look how diverse men and women are.

Names – When Laura, Anna, and Lisa get together they call each other Laura, Anna, and Lisa. When Mark, Steve, and Tom hang out they affectionately refer to each other as bro, dude, man, or homey.

Eating Out – After dinner when men get the check they all throw in $20 even though the bill is only $32.50. When women get the check, out come the pocket calculators.

Money – Men pay $2 for a $1 item that they need. Women pay $1 for a $2 item that they don't need. 'Buy One Get One' is a woman's motto.

Bathrooms – A man has 4 items in the bathroom: a toothbrush, shaving cream, razor, and deodorant. A woman has 154 items. A man cannot identify most of these items.

Arguments – Women have the last word in any argument. Anything men say after that is the beginning of a new argument.

Cats – Women love cats. Men say they love cats, but when women aren't looking, men kick cats.

The Future – Women worry about the future until they get a husband. A man never worries about the future until they get a wife.

Success – A successful man makes more money than his wife can spend. A successful woman is one who can find such a man.

Dressing Up – Most women dress up to go shopping, water the plants, empty the garbage, answer the phone, read a book, and get the mail. Men dress up for weddings and funerals.

Appearance – Women wake up as gorgeous as they went to bed. Men somehow deteriorate during the night.

Children – A woman knows all about her children. She knows about school schedules, doctor appointments, best friends, favorite foods, secret fears, and hopes and dreams. A man is vaguely aware that there are some short people living in the house.

Mistakes – Any married man should forget his mistakes. There's no use in two people remembering the same thing.

Marriage – A woman marries a man expecting he will change, but he doesn't. A man marries a woman expecting that she won't change, and she does.

Simply put, men and women are worlds apart. Rocket science is irrelevant at this point. In fact, men and women are so uniquely different, it seems illogical they could be compatible at all. Ironically, social norm suggests that opposites attract in the dating phase. Yet, it's incompatibility and irreconcilable differences that so often precipitate divorce. So which is it; opposites attract or opposites divide?

In order to further investigate these theories, I actually logged onto a few dating and marriage websites. However, to fully indulge my curiosity, these sites required me to create real personality profiles in order to complete the process. Therefore, I eventually backed out. However, my findings up to that point were very interesting. All of these sites require very lengthy aptitude and attitudinal tests to produce clear results in areas of compatibility. The survey questions on these sites thoroughly screen applicants to adequately sort and place them in the precise category of people who suit them as a possible mate. Some sites strongly suggest that they can find the "perfect match." The areas of compatibility combined from all sites I researched break down into these basic eight basic categories.

Emotional Disposition: What is your overall temperament and attitude toward life, and how do you naturally respond to your environment (both good and bad)?

Social Preference: Who do you like to be with on a regular basis? What people/social groups do you tend to gravitate toward? Do you have hidden or undiscussed prejudices toward certain people?

Motivational Factors: What energizes, stimulates and motivates you? What makes you "tick?" Who do you need around you to succeed in life? Who drains and demotivates you.

Physical Priority: How important is physical appearance? What priority do you place on sexual attraction in the relationship? How do you rate others based on their appearance?

Relational Dynamics: How do you relate to others. Do you have good people skills? Are you self-centered or *other's* focused? Do you like the spotlight or do you spot others in their light?

Life Experience: What common interests will help bring you together. What activities are important to you that will help bond the relationship ongoing? Do you want that significant someone to like mostly what you like?

Family History: How does your family background work into the relationship? Does your family experience and upbringing strongly influence who you are? What importance do your parents have and what role will they play in the future of your relationship? Are you far removed from them, closely connected, or somewhere in the middle? Do your siblings reflect who you are in some way? Did your family history prepare you for being able to form a long lasting and healthy relationship?

Core Values: What are the most important things in your life? What ideals are you unwilling to compromise? What is your guiding force? Does religion, ethics, morals and convictions frame your general perspective? What do you exist for? Dow you have a clearly defined purpose and pursuit? Does eternity weigh on your priorities?

In each of these categories, an extensive list of questions are asked to determine *who you are* before you are matched. As a general rule, these types of applications are difficult to answer truthfully and honestly. This is because we normally answer personality surveys based on how we see ourselves versus how we really are. Also, many times we do not fully understand the questions presented. Therefore, they are often answered too quickly or even randomly. No survey is full proof.[11] Also, research suggests that your friends may better see you for who you really are. This is because we are often objects of our own perception. Our friends and close associates have a 360 degree view. They observe us when we aren't observing ourselves. Typically, when we keep tabs on our own behavior it is controlled or manipulated to fit the situation. Simply put, we are most ourselves when we aren't *trying* to be ourselves.[12] Thus, in order to more accurately answer personality based surveys, maybe we should have our friends submit them for us. Multiple choice questions are not necessarily adequate at categorizing our multiple issues; they often only further reveal them. Truthfully, much of what singles submit on these types of websites does not reflect the totality of who they truly are. Rather, it's more of a self-defined or self-refined image of how they see themselves, or more importantly, how they *want* to see themselves.

Now, before I continue, I am not trying to find fault or devalue dating websites. In fact, some sites are even Christian based and were created out of a motivation to help solve the relationship, compatibility, and marriage-divorce dilemma. I'm simply pointing out that no matter how well you try to find the perfect mate, you're still going to discover many imperfections in one another as time goes on, and only Grace will equip you to deal with them as they arise in marriage.

Another factor we must consider, is while personality tests may reveal a facsimile of one's personality, it is impossible for them to fully reveal one's true character. Real character is exposed by the pressures of life's circumstances not by multiple choice questions. Character is everything in a person's life and cannot be discovered on a web page. While personality is surface, it is character that reveals the depths of who we are. The complexities and challenges of relationships, especially in marriage, will expose the real you. Deep inside, most of us would love to enter marriage with the curtains pulled back on one another so we could see everything about our mate. That's why so many are tempted and drawn to these websites in attempts to manage the baggage before it is *unpacked*. We would like to eliminate all the problems in marriage before they occur. However, the longer you stay married to someone, even after finding someone on these sites, you may still be taken aback. Why? Because change is inevitable. I know a friend who was matched with someone on a Christian dating website. Yet, after two years of dating they put things on *hold*. My friend said, *"I have to be who I am, and if she can't fully accept me, then it's best that we just be friends."* After two years of dating they discovered they were not as compatible as the website suggested. In a very practical way, this illustrates that compatibility is much more of a relational issue than it is a cognitive control issue.

Something interesting to add here is that most major dating and marriage websites suggest that there are certain *factors* in our past or present history that will almost *guarantee* some to have a low probability of success in a relationship.[20] For instance, what if certain clients are discovered to have had issues such as a history of addictions, criminal records, or emotional conditions which chronically disrupted their life? What if tests conclude that some even have a tendency toward unreliability, irresponsibility, or erratic behavior? In some cases these clients are recognized as serious "red flags" and the sites categorized them accordingly.[15] The sites even recommended a delay in getting married. In my case, I came from a very broken family before my adoption and although I'm a relatively healthy person, both emotionally and spiritually, I still didn't have everything *worked out* in my past before I got married. Truth is, I've always been a work in progress (as is every other person on the planet). I still have issues that only Grace can atone for. This means if I would have opted to enter the online dating arena, according to some online dating sites, I may have found myself incompatible with my wife. Thus we would have never been matched. Truthfully, my wife is the only one for me and probably the only one who could put up with me. Her strengths compliment my weaknesses and in many cases, caress my weaknesses. The same goes for my strengths to my wife's weaknesses. Grace says—when and where I am weak, Christ is strong for me (2 Corinthians 12:9-11). This is the model for all true compatibility in marriage.

What about romantic compatibility or chemistry? In the dating phase, singles may assume that they are making sensible decisions about who is compatible with them as they browse profiles. Yet, they are still unable to get an accurate sense of their romantic compatibility until they actually meet the other person face-to-face, or at least by webcam. Consequently, it's unlikely that you will make a better decision whether you browse profiles for 20 hours or 20 minutes.[15] How can you know if you are truly compatible with someone based on mathematical algorithms? God did not design people to be matched by metadata. Although some dating websites claim to have developed a sophisticated matching algorithm that can find you a uniquely compatible mate, it is not supported by any credible evidence.[15]

From a scientific perspective, dating websites fail to produce bona fide evidence that fully convince clients of their "expertise" and qualifications.[15] In other words, the people operating these sites may not necessarily be qualified or nearly insightful enough to know who is truly compatible. They mostly base their findings from meta-data conclusions.[15] And what about the flaw factor? Are those that facilitate and filter these online applications and tests emotionally healthy enough to do so in a proper manner? Just because one may have a degree in relational therapy doesn't necessarily mean they are capable to appropriately administer sophisticated online procedures, nor appropriate the matching process altogether.

More importantly, are these online tests based on any kind of Biblical truth and guidance? Is there appropriate accountability for online assessment. Does the applicant have trusted and loving counseling while completing the process? This raises the question: should flawed people be pairing flawed people? When you think of it this way, there is a good chance that the results of online matching systems could be potentially more risky and even disastrous? Truth is, relational management websites can potentially give a false sense of security. Thus, couples may buy into the idea that they are being pared with someone like them. Yet, when they finally meet that *someone*, they make every effort to guard themselves from the other seeing their "negative side." However, sooner or later all will be revealed. There's no hiding. Only through entering the crucible of a real relationship do we discover our true selves and allow God to refine our temperaments, align our hearts, and sanctify our souls.

No matter how you meet or who you marry, things will arise you never knew in the other person; and as you grow older the changes will never stop evolving. As time rolls on, you are even going to surprise yourself. Marriage is the union of two imperfect people joined together by a perfect God, not by algorithms. No website can fully prepare you for all the complexities of marriage. My grandparents were happily married for over 50 years and it didn't take a website to bring them together or help them stay together. They weathered the storms of life in marriage not because they had a deeply intimate foreknowledge of one another, but rather a resolve to stay together and love each other deeply no matter what they discovered along the way.

Essentially, when you married your spouse, you married all their life experiences including their hang ups, let downs, parents, sisters, brothers, aunts, uncles, teachers, pets, friends, secrets, etc. No website can uncover all of this. With marriage comes baggage and everyone has baggage (folded, wrinkled, clean, and smelly). Sometimes from the beginning of a relationship (and in particular marriage) we have this idea that our mate should have already worked everything out by the time we've met. This is a total misconception. *The good news is that while your family history, and every other relationship you've ever had affects your perspective of marriage, it does not have to determine the outcome of your marriage.*

At some point, couples are going to discover areas of brokenness in one another; and the truth is sometimes there's no fully preparing you for it. This is why we don't need compatibility guides in marriage. We need compatibility Grace! For most of us who didn't have the help of certain websites, we should be *done for*. To be honest, although I'm saved, and my past is completely under the blood, I still exemplify negative behavior patterns from time to time that emerge from my past. However, by Grace, I am continuously being sanctified from my past.

Grace is the only thing that makes us compatible to God. There is no reason on earth why God should be drawn to us but He was. So much so, that he sent his best to rescue and redeem us. God didn't require that we take a test to see if we were compatible for salvation; he simply sent His Son. There's no other explanation for it. It's all by Grace! Nothing more and nothing less. I am not saying that dating and marriage websites aren't somewhat helpful in the process of the modern dating dilemma. There is evidence of *solid* matchups in some online services and have actually been successful at pairing couples. However, extensive research still suggests that profile browsing is no more effective than finding love the old fashioned way.[20] Truth is, no matter how you meet someone, the longer you stay together you will inevitably encounter the same issues common to all relationships. In every marriage there are highs, lows, excitement, boredom, predictability, shock, disappointments, questions, regrets, hurts, joy, sadness, likes, dislikes, and even serious and starkly contrasting areas of incompatibility. The list goes on and on.

One caution to singles… During the dating phase you need to be especially sensitive to the Holy Spirit. He will search the deep things in your life and reveal the red flags in your relationships (1 Corinthians 2:10). Sensitivity to God is necessary in order to discern whether or not a person is either *right* or *wrong* for you. *You must fully lean into God before fully launching out into marriage.* This will prevent much heartache later on. Singles pursuing marriage must rely on God's wisdom regarding whom to marry. This being said, people are human and sometimes make wrong decisions even with the purest of motives and intentions. Also, after saying, "I do," sometimes people change for the worse. That's why it is extremely important to be honest with yourself and listen to God, trusted friends and wise counsel in the matter of marriage. When you marry someone, you don't get to fix them or opt out once things get tough. You have to accept that person and make a lasting commitment to love and stay with them. There is no optional escape plan in marriage.

No matter how you slice it, real relationships are risky and there is a great chance that you won't be as compatible with your mate as you first thought. That's O.K. For a long lasting and fulfilling marriage we don't need compatibility, we need UNITY!

So let's talk about that some more...

Chapter 9

UNITY MAKES
THE DIFFERENCE

I have come to the conclusion that compatibility isn't really the main issue of marriage. It's Unity! Unity is more important in marriage than compatibility. Unity is what makes the difference. As we have previously mentioned, compatibility has become much too major an issue in marriage, so much so that couples want to call it quits when they *seem* to no longer have anything in common. Marriages teeter on the brink of divorce when the differences begin to interfere with love and intimacy. Couples struggle to love and accept one another through their emerging personality and character flaws. We must look through the eyes of Grace for our spouses just as God sees us. God doesn't accept us based on our past, our character, our personality, or compatibility. He accepts us based on the finished work of Christ! Grace doesn't match us by our performance based on any area of social, physical, or emotional criteria. *We are not joined to Christ because of compatibility but because of the cross.* The cross symbolizes Christ's sacrifice and commitment to love us at all costs. The cross is the image of intersection: it's God's perfection intersecting with our imperfection. When my wife and I got married, we literally intersected with each other. Everything she is merged with everything I am. In fact, it was more like a collision. Two worlds collided! That's what happened when Jesus came into my life. Heaven collided with earth and Heaven won! Grace won!

When my wife married me she got all of me including my complications. Marriage is one complicated person being married to another complicated person. In mathematical terms complicated + complicated = complications. However, marriage isn't logical or fundamentally mathematical. Love cannot be controlled in a laboratory of tests and experiments. Both people in the marriage relationship are fundamentally flawed, not just because of their past, but because marriage creates a consistent norm of changes and challenges. Not only do couples compliment one another; they often complicate one another. With the blessing of marriage comes the battle of marriage. However, rather than fight against each other, a Grace made marriage fights together—to stay together. Commitment trumps compatibility. My wife and I can fully attest to this. In areas of emotional stability and aptitude we both rank quite differently. However, my wife and I have fully accepted that marriage doesn't complete us. Only Christ completes us.

"So you also are complete through your union with Christ, who is the head over every ruler and authority." (Colossians 2:10 NLT)

Contrary to popular opinion, compatibility doesn't necessarily guarantee completeness. Many couples that marry have many common interests and similarities yet still divorce. Being married doesn't mean you're buddies, it means you're married. Truth is, no person is completely compatible with another person. Although couples may have many *compatibilities,* sometimes all it takes is one area of incompatibility and its grounds for major dispute and division. There are many couples that have many common interests. Yet, often because of just one or two insignificant differences major division ensues. Couples who live under the legalistic umbrella of compatibility will hold each other accountable to the standard they set for themselves. When you base your marriage off of compatibility dimensions, they eventually become compatibility standards. Once again, a legalistic marriage lives by demands, standards and expectations. The main difference between a Law based marriage and a Grace based marriage is while one expects, the other accepts.

Often couples attempt to discover significance through one another's areas of compatibility. Its, if we're compatible then we'll be satisfied. However, Grace meets all four criteria of our essential needs: love, significance, acceptance, and forgiveness. In a Grace made marriage, we model these and liberally grant them. How can a marriage not thrive in an environment like this? Many women are looking for the perfect husband. They want a man that's rich, tall, handsome, romantic, powerful and loving. My response to this is, *"Hang in there sister, Jesus is coming very soon."* So often when people are looking to marry, the very opposite of what they are looking for will present themselves. Interestingly, I've also found that opposites actually do attract, especially when Grace is involved.

The truth is, God is not compatible with us, but He gave His own Son to make us one with Him. Jesus is our opposite in every way. He came from a mansion. We came from a prison. He walked on streets of gold; we were lying in the gutter. Yet, his Grace lifted us from the gutter-most and raised us to the uttermost. I've seen God's Grace work through my wife to help bring out the best in me when all that was there was the worst in me.

The Grace of God through my wife has served as a powerful means of transformation in my life. For the most part, Sherri and I are opposites. We have many of the traditional differences that most men and women have. Sherri likes Hallmark movies, I like action movies with explosions, shooting, fighting, intense drama, and action sequences. I like the thermostat at 65 degrees year-round; she needs sweat shirts and 20 blankets to stay warm. My creativity combined with my A.D.D. inspires spontaneity and last minute planning. Sherri likes maps, instructions, and detailed plans ahead of time. My wife likes spicy food; I like starchy food. I like to stay up late; she *turns-in* early. I like modern design; she likes classic, French, and Victorian style. I like to dress trendy; she dresses conservatively. I like to discuss theology; she loves to change the subject. The list goes on. Yet, we're still happily together as one because Grace is fully at play.

For Sherri and I, our backgrounds are very different, and the longer we stay married, the longer we discover these differences. In the beginning it was hard to notice these things because we simply lived off of blind love. However, longevity in marriage opens your eyes. As the differences have emerged over time (and in some cases evolved) it has challenged us and sometimes even stretched us to our limit. Yet, Grace has no limits. Fortunately, our core values and commitment to love God and one another are so strong the differences that have surfaced are like throwing a pebble at a mountain. In other words, the differences between my wife and are so insignificant compared to our deep and growing love for one another and our steadfast commitment to dwell together in unity. Our love stands the test of time. As the old song says, "Ain't no mountain high enough." Love truly conquers all and trumps all the differences. Sherri and I truly have a fulfilling and happy marriage because, for the last 27 years, we have both lived by the premise, *"I can't change you; but I still want to chase you."*

In a Grace made marriage, love is the focus. When you're driving down the road you don't pay attention to the flies that land on the windshield; you keep your eyes on the road. The vision for your marriage is much bigger than the flies (little irritations and perceived flaws) that land in your marriage. *Being different in marriage doesn't have to divide the marriage.* Differences in a couple's relationship can serve to make the marriage more interesting. I once heard a college professor say that when he came home to his wife, he didn't want a student, or a fellow teacher to be waiting on him. He wanted a wife. When couples are connected by an enduring faith in God and a love for one another, the differences can make life more intriguing than fatiguing. Incompatibility can actually promote stability. A carpenter's work-horse doesn't stand on legs that all point in the same direction. Quite the contrary. Each leg faces outward in opposite directions to support the heavy workload that is often laid upon it. Likewise, a couple's differences can serve as a support to withstand the outside pressure that can often put stress on and compromise the relationship. It's fascinating to me how much Sherri and I are madly in love with each other and yet have so many differences. Truth is, you will never find anyone the same as you. Men and women are opposite in the very DNA encoded in them. The fact that a man and a woman dwell together in marriage is proof that opposites do attract. Perspective is everything in marriage. You can see your differences as dividing features or attracting features. It's tempting to get hung up and strung up on all the differences, or you can learn to appreciate the uniqueness of your mate. It's all a matter of choice and perspective.

Puzzles pieces are all shaped differently, yet they are created to perfectly interconnect. In the massive complexity of the jigsaw puzzle of marriage, all the pieces of who each of you are were perfectly designed to create a beautiful mosaic of what God created your marriage to be. When you critically analyze each piece of the puzzle by itself it can be… well… quite puzzling. You question where the piece belongs and wonder how it fits into the overall scheme of the picture. However, the longer you question it's relevance and no longer trust that it contributes to the overall picture, you may discard the piece and even stop working on the puzzle all together. Puzzle pieces, though totally opposite from one another, are actually completely compatible. It's the opposite shape that makes them fit together.

Sometimes your mate's unique *shape* or *puzzle piece* doesn't seem to fit in the temporary picture of your marriage. Doubt sets in. Questions arise. Regrets begin to form. Concerns weigh heavy. You must understand that it takes a lifetime for the puzzle picture of marriage to form. You won't be able to see the full picture of marriage unless you stay in it for the long hall. Sometimes it will seem the puzzle is incomplete and that some pieces are missing. Keep building the puzzle together and enjoy the process. Don't give up. My wife and I have been married almost three decades and just when I didn't think it could get anymore interesting, we discover another piece of the puzzle. We've chosen to continue allowing God to fit us together. Rather than try to reshape the pieces of our lives by cutting or repainting them (criticizing or changing them), we have chosen to accept the way the piece looks and allow it to find it's place in our relationship. So many couples try to change one another rather than ask God how their differences can fit into the overall scope of their marriage.

The bottom line is you may be different from one another but you can still be ONE! A Grace made marriage gives permanence and structure to a couple's love no matter the differences. It's a way to tell one another that no matter how different we are, or how much we disagree, we're still in this together. We are ONE! On a much deeper level, it doesn't' matter where you've been, what you've done or who you were, or what the compatibility tests show. Rather, it's who you ARE now and where you are going, or more importantly, where WE are going together! It's saying, *"I love you regardless of our differences, and I want to be a lifetime part of what God is doing in you and where He's taking you. If I'm going anywhere, it's with YOU!"* A Grace made marriage is not based on a marriage rulebook, scorebook, or compatibility standard to keep. Aren't you glad God didn't give us a long compatibility test before we met him? I'm grateful for the Grace that calls me loved, adored, redeemed, perfect, spotless, completely favored, approachable, lovable, and whole. God never views us as incompatible with him. When we are joined to him we are ONE with him (1 Corinthians 6:17). Likewise, when couples are joined together in marriage, the Spirit of God makes them one, completely irrelevant of their common interests or areas of compatibility.

"And the two will become one flesh.' So they
are no longer two, but one flesh."
(Mark 10:8 NIV)

The word *become* in this passage in the Greek means *esomai* which means to *sojourn*. Becoming one is not only an initial act at the onset of marriage, but is an ongoing journey, an adventure if you will. As each day passes we are *becoming one* with the person we married. The powerful thing about a Grace made marriage is it gives us the ability to walk with who our mate IS without stumbling on what our mate is NOT. Grace grants each other an atmosphere in which each can grow. It is a common search for the good and the beautiful. It is not only marrying the right partner, but BEING the right partner. Instead of constantly pointing to the other person to be right for us, we should live to be the right person for them. This would fix much of the compatibility problems in marriage. Pride keeps us from conceding, changing, and lovingly compromising to the benefit of the other. If we pridefully stand our ground as individuals, we may actually loose ground in marriage. An unwillingness to budge eventually creates a grudge. Yet, a Grace made marriage says, *"I'm going to stop trying to fix you and let the Holy Spirit work in your life."* When we attempt to fix compatibility issues in one another, we tend to fail at it even worse than if we didn't try fixing them at all. Sure, there are things about ourselves that we will not be able to change regarding compatibility. However, it is honorable that we compromise at some things and even attempt to involve ourselves in the other's interests as best we can, taking on activities, and hobbies that the other enjoys. This is just good form in marriage. However, working on compatibility at marriage is not how to have a successful marriage or save a marriage. Looking at your partner as a finished work is the foundation of a Grace-made marriage. No matter the areas of incompatibility, we are truly complete in Christ. God didn't give us our mates to change them. He gave us our mates to enjoy them.

"And the Lord God said, "It isn't good for man to be alone; I will make a companion for him, a helper suited to his needs... "This is it!" Adam exclaimed. "She is part of my own bone and flesh! Her name is 'woman' because she was taken out of a man." (Genesis 2:18-23 TLB)

Notice how elated Adam is when he sees Eve. He doesn't see her as a problem to be solved but the perfect solution for his dilemma. She is exactly what he needs. The Hebrew word for the phrase *"helper suited to his needs"* is *Ezer* which means *divine*

170

help. It means to rescue, save, and be strong for someone. This does not imply subordination, but rather cooperation. My wife is God's divine help in my life, and all the more so since she has been regenerated by God's Grace. The word *companion* in this verse is a related word to *compatible*. Without compromising the text, this verse could actually read that *"God made a helper that was totally and perfectly compatible for Adam."* One translation says that God gave him a *"helper fit for him."* That means that God gave Adam the perfect fit for his life. Our mates are more perfect for us than we realize. In marriage, all our similarities and differences help one another. That's how God designed your mate for you. The word *help* means to lift, to make better, to bring out the good, to support, to embellish, to more fully enhance, to strengthen, to sharpen, to improve, to build, and to edify. Wow!

The real issue here isn't compatibility as much as it is unity. You can be totally unified and at the same time be very different than one another. This is because, while compatibility takes equal relational effort, unity is a work only the Holy Spirit can bring about. Unity is actually a miracle. Think of the word UNITY as a sentence: *You and I are tied.* Nothing can separate us. We are one!

When we are joined as one in marriage we mustn't view our marriage as compatible or incompatible. We must see ourselves as ONE. My wife's "areas of concern" are now my areas of concern, not just the *good* stuff, but the *bad* stuff as well. She is mine and I am hers. When I became one with Christ, I took on all his perfection and he took on all my imperfection. I got what he deserved and he got what I deserved. We are one. The same is of marriage. We take on one another's imperfections as well as areas of incompatibility. You've heard that in marriage, *"What's yours is mine and what's mine is yours."* We mostly equivocate this to our earthly possessions, but rule it out on everything else. Truth is, your mate's consistencies and inconsistencies are yours alike. These are not just your mate's *areas* to work out; it's BOTH of your areas to work out. When your wife struggles, you struggle. When your mate suffers, you suffer. When your mate succeeds, you succeed. You are one with each other. That's true unity in marriage.

"And if one member suffers, all the members suffer with it; if *one* member is honored, all the members rejoice with it." (1 Corinthians 12:26 NASB)

Of course the above passage is directly referring to the church, However, the theme of unity is just as applicable in the marriage relationship. After all, churches are made of families and families are made of marriages. The marriage is the core cell of the body of Christ and must exemplify unity in it's purest form. Unity is the key principle at work here. Choosing to dwell together in love, regardless of isolated incompatibility issues, demonstrates true unity. This type of bond produces the power to overcome every obstacle in marriage in spite of complications, past history, strong differences in opinion, or personal outlook. Unity produces the anointing and the anointing breaks the yoke of bondage that Satan tries to put on our marriages (Psalms 133; Isaiah 10:27). The devil's schemes against marriage are no match for a loving couple unified in holy matrimony. Unity is stronger than compatibility. Again, through unity, not only do we take on one another's good qualities, but also the not-so-good qualities. We are One. Sometimes when your mate is demonstrating a negative side-effect of their history, it is tempting to say, *"That's your problem."* However, in marriage, as in Christ's relationship to us, he doesn't abandon us to work on our problems and then invite us back when they are solved. Quite the contrary. Our problems are HIS problems. He loves us and has joined himself to us. Likewise, in a Grace made marriage, a couple's love for one another overcomes the differences that have the potential to undermine the marriage. After almost three decades, my wife and I are still together and more in love than ever. Unity has truly made the difference in our marriage.

What kind of world would we have if music only had a melody. What makes a beautiful melody even more beautiful is the counter harmony part. Two distinct lines, with different pitches, intervals, and tonal directions, yet simultaneously moving in the same unified direction... Forward! What a beautiful example of a Grace made marriage—two different hearts moving in sync to make exquisite music. My wife and I have been composing a masterpiece for almost three decades. Sometimes the music is in development, dramatic, chaotic, and full of dissonance. Yet somehow, like a musical masterpiece, it eventually resolves to it's original theme... a Grace made marriage.

"He makes all things beautiful in his time."
(Ecclesiastes 3:11)

Chapter 10

THE 'D' WORD

Yes, we need to talk about it. It's a word we're never supposed use in marriage… Divorce! D.I.V.O.R.C.E. stands for division in values obscuring relational commitment and enjoyment.[8] Divorce is a rampant reality in the world we live in. The divorce rate is soaring to the extent that many churches are struggling to adequately address and minister to an ever growing number of troubled marriages. In fact, data from Barna Research suggests that born again Christians are statistically indistinguishable from the national average on the matter of divorce. Among those who have declared their wedding vows, one out of three have been divorced at least once (Barna Research 2013). Divorce is not just a problem; it's a plague!

The single basic element in all of life is an atom. It holds every living thing together. The most destructive thing in the world is the atomic bomb. It involves the splitting of a single atom. When an atom is split, it wreaks havoc on everything. Nothing survives. Devastation! Marriage is the single most important component of the family and society as a whole. When you split a marriage, destruction results. I've heard it said by those who have walked through divorce that it is the closest thing to hell on earth. Lives are often destroyed, children are uprooted and deeply scarred, homes are lost and hearts are broken. Divorce is very painful and ugly. This is why God hates divorce (Malachi 2:16). However, even though God hates divorce, he doesn't hate the divorcee. God hates sin, but he doesn't hate the sinner. God hates sickness but he doesn't hate those who are sick. Divorce is not the unforgivable sin. God has compassion on those who are going through divorce but hates what it does to them.

God didn't create divorce; he created marriage. That's why Satan wants to destroy marriages. A unified marriage that puts Christ at the center is a dangerous threat to the kingdom of darkness. It is a model that demonstrates the love and Grace of

God and is a perfect example and shining light of Christ's loving relationship to his bride, the church (Ephesians 5:21-33). Satan schemes to tear apart anything that even closely resembles the redeeming work of the cross and the resurrection. He wants to discredit, slander, and bring to ruin what God created (John 10:10). Yet, even though the enemy may have tried to destroy your marriage, the good news is Jesus has come to bring LIFE! He can resuscitate what is dying and resurrect what is dead. You may say, *"Not my marriage! You have NO idea!"* There is never an exceptional case beyond the saving power of Jesus. He is the resurrection and the life. It is not his will for you to lose your marriage. No marriage conflict is too difficult for him (Jeremiah 32:17). You say, *"It's impossible,"* but with God ALL things are possible (Matthew 19:26). Even If your marriage is dangling by a thread, HOPE is right there to catch you!

You may be looking for a way out or hope you will find something in these pages that will condone your desire to file for divorce. This book is not to condone divorce but rather help marriages stay together through God's Grace. However, I cannot deny that in a broken world, some marriages don't make it. Divorce happens, and I do not judge or condemn couples who have walked this difficult path. The purpose of this book is to help your marriage survive but also give much Grace if your marriage doesn't work out. Please know that divorce isn't the end. You are loved by God, and his Grace is available to restore you and help you begin again. There is more than enough Grace for you. However, just because divorce happens, doesn't mean that it should happen or has to happen to you. The Bible encourages reconciliation where possible. This is the ideal. Yet, we don't live in an ideal world. We live in a REAL world. God's ideal has always been that we should remain committed to the marriage covenant. Divorce is a departure from God's ideal. Yet, in a fallen world, some marriage relationships actually get worse the longer they stay together. However, the key is not just to *stay* together but take *steps* together to make marriage work. The preservation of a marriage depends on two wills, and one partner can sometimes end a marriage unilaterally against the other's will. It can happen to anyone regardless of position, hours spent in prayer, counseling, or pleading. Despite the most stringent of doctrinal positions and theologies, divorce can and does happen.[6] There are so many cases where marriage seems irreconcilable. These cases are not just isolated to circumstances involving spousal abuse, child endangerment, and repeated infidelity. There are many other sobering issues surrounding troubled marriages that may lead to divorce if forgiveness, repentance, and restoration is not achieved.

Some scriptures even seem to give reasonable understanding and leniency for divorce in difficult cases (Matthew 19:19). However, the Bible as a whole does not ultimately condone divorce as a full proof solution to the marriage dilemma. Yet, we shouldn't flippantly use these verses to endorse divorce or run away at the first sign of trouble. At the same time, we should not use other verses to judge and condemn those who have been unable to resolve the severe and life altering difficulties within their marriages. Jesus commands us to forgive one another, but he also strongly instructs us not to judge one another (Matthew 18:21-22; Matthew 7:1; Luke 6:37)

All being said, God's Word points couples toward mutual forgiveness and restoration. No matter how many times spouses fail each another, they can choose to forgive through the power of the Resurrection. When we take action to work on our marriages instead of run, we allow Grace to release it's redemptive power. Persevering in a difficult marriage isn't easy, but your marriage is worth fighting for. Marriage is not for the faint of heart. Yet, our weakness is the perfect opportunity for Christ to show himself strong through our marriages (2 Corinthians 12:9-11).

As difficult and painful as your marriage may be, it is God's will to heal it. However, if you've tried everything to forgive, and your spouse is still unwilling to work with you towards mutual reconciliation, then you may have done all that you can do. Just know, that even if you are a victim of a struggling marriage or ultimately a divorce, there is abundant Grace to forgive. No matter the pain, rejection, betrayal, or grief, there is mammoth strength and courage available in Christ to forgive. Many marriages don't experience healing and miracles because they've given up saying, *"I've been too hurt to be hurt again. It's over!"* This is plausible. I don't fault those who have reached their limit of abuse, hardness of heart, betrayal, infidelity, and are irreversibly calloused toward their mate. However, even in these cases, there is NO heartache with which Jesus doesn't identify, and there is no hurt he cannot heal. After all, Jesus is our Healer.

The marriage covenant makes two people into one (Genesis 2:24; Mark 10:8). Marriage is not a decision to be considered frivolously or foolishly. When God Himself wills for two hearts to become one, they must enter the marriage joyfully and soberly at the same time. It is a serious covenant. They are being united by the Holy Spirit and are to be bound together for life.

"Therefore what God has joined together, let no one separate." (Mark 10:9 NIV)

God joins people together in marriage and what he has joined together, we should cooperate with him to keep it together. However, God gave us free will, and although he does join couples together, we can miss out on his purposes if we refuse to allow Him to work in our lives and marriages. Pride can win over. Know that storms will come against your marriage and threaten it. You can allow the storms inside the marriage, or you can ask God for the Grace to keep them out.

Important to the topic of God joining people together in marriage, we must also realize that God does not always join every couple together. Sadly, many people marry outside of God's perfect will. Just because people are married by a judge or a preacher with a full-blown ceremony, does not mean that God initiates, orchestrates, or endorses every marriage. He doesn't necessarily approve of every decision to get married. Not all marriages are holy matrimonies. Some are actually unholy matrimonies. The marriage ceremony doesn't guarantee God's consent. Though many decide to get married, they can still be absolutely out of the will of God. Couples all too often marry in direct opposition to God's plan. It is simply not God's best for some couples to come together. This may explain why many marriages fail. God was not in it from the beginning. The marriage covenant was entered lightly without prayer and counsel. When marriage fails, many legalistically and automatically assume that God endorsed the union and thus disapproves of the divorce. To this judgments arise. However, we must be very understanding and gracious to couples who are in this particular dilemma. Many marriages end in bitter divorce because God was not the one who drew them together by his Spirit. A great number of people snub honesty from close friends, reject wise counsel, ignore loving parental involvement, refuse community support, and decline pastoral advising and guidance when considering marriage. Some even marry out of adamant and callous rebellion to clear scriptural authority, often resulting in much marital grief and ultimately divorce. This is why marriage must be entered humbly, cautiously, and prayerfully, laying aside all prideful and selfish resistance. The first and most important safeguard against divorce is to marry in alignment to God's will. Again, please understand that I do not couples in contempt if their marriage has failed. Separation and divorce happens, and when it does there is redeeming Grace available to heal and start over. We live in a broken world, and some marriages simply end after they've tried everything to make it. Due to scriptural ignorance and legalistic fervor, some stand in judgment of those walking through divorce. However, only God has the final word on broken marriages, and we should never judge people who have determined their marriage is irreconcilable.

IMPORTANT NOTE: Sometimes separation and divorce can actually be an act of mercy and grace where the emotional wellbeing and safety of the spouse and children are at risk. If you are in a situation where there is physical or emotional abuse, please seek further help from law enforcement, the church, pastors, licensed counselors, or social services. God does not want you to remain in harm's way (1 Corinthians 7:15).

The Apostle Paul specifically addresses the issues of marriage and divorce. He goes back and forth from what the Lord says, and at the same time adds his own commentary and personal opinion throughout (1 Corinthians 7:10-17). Paul is not condoning divorce here. However, because of the complexity of relational brokenness, and in some cases pride and hardness of heart, he provides some leniency for divorce and remarriage. He states that if a Christian has a non-believing spouse and they do not want to divorce, the believer must not divorce them or send them away. However, if the non-believer wants to leave, Paul advises the believing spouse to release them. Furthermore, he states that the believing spouse is not bound in such cases (1 Corinthians 7:15). However, nowhere in this passage does Paul say if you are simply "unhappy" that it's permissible to divorce. You may ask, *"Well, God wants me to be happy, doesn't he?"* Absolutely! God wants you to be happy. However, if you leave your spouse, but cleave to bitterness in your heart, refusing to forgive, you'll never be happy. Many divorce but never truly let go and find spiritual and emotional healing. Divorce is not a guarantee that all will be well. Few divorces end agreeably and amicably. Many use divorce as a weapon to hurt their spouse, yet end up hurting themselves in the long run. *Many couples separate but never fully reparate.* Divorcees may pursue new relationships but may also fail at maintaining healthy ones if they are still ensnared in the bitterness of their previous marriages. *Marital dissolution does not necessarily mean marital resolution.* While it may be challenging to love a difficult person, it does not necessarily establish grounds for divorce. In fact, it's an opportunity for God to teach and develop within us sincere forgiveness, tolerance, forbearance, patience, long-suffering, gentleness, meekness, and all the other Godly attributes that the Spirit produces in our lives. God allows for Paul's personal commentaries and advising on marriage to be included in Biblical cannon for the purpose of helping make sense of the difficult nature of divorce and how to handle it appropriately. In the scheme of life, there will be situations that allow for much Grace regarding special conditions due to irreconcilable severities. It is not always black and white. For all intents and purposes, the goal is Biblical balance. Simply put, divorce is not a free-for-all decision. However, in cases where divorce happens due to hardness of heart, scriptures give some leniency to the church because of such circumstances. At the time that 1 Corinthians was written, Paul was carefully addressing and even boldly confronting several serious, complex and somewhat unconventional situations surrounding the church at Corinth regarding matters of divorce and remarriage. It is important to note that there were incestuous relations and other explicitly overt perversions and practices occurring in the local church there. Things were totally out of control. Paul prayerfully sought to bring balance to a volatile situation. All of this serves to reiterate that marriage must not be taken lightly, nor should we judge others where divorce is imminent.

One caveat here, Some couples stay together because of legalistic upbringing, but nevertheless, remain miserable, refusing to work on their marriage. Pervasive tension and civil unrest persists in the home. Simply staying together is not enough. Staying committed to working on the relationship is much more important if the marriage is to survive. Couples should not just settle to live as roommates under one roof just because of legalistic pressures and fear of the shame of divorce. Couples who want to see their marriage not only survive but THRIVE must take action to build a healthy marriage.

Sadly, many have simply chosen to walk out on their spouses for the typical reasons that are often just part of the ups and downs of normal married life. Spouses become weary of the constant bickering, resentment, bitterness, and careless, irresponsible behaviors. They are *so over* the criticisms and hateful remarks. On top of that there's the prolonged communication stalemates, a true lack of sexual intimacy, deep emotional disconnect, financial pressures, opposite career paths, major differences on how to discipline children, and the list goes on. All too often, marriages end on the common note of irreconcilable differences, or more accurately stated, the differences they are *unwilling* to reconcile. It's, *"Enough is enough. I'm done!"*

Many settle for the common misconception that says, *"God doesn't want me to be unhappy."* Truthfully, sometimes my wife and I have been unhappy in our marriage. However, even though we may not always see eye to eye, we've made a commitment to walk heart to heart and hand in hand even through our most challenging seasons. Since we're on the subject of holding hands, here's a powerful word of advice to couples: Never stop holding hands! In all my research, some of the most commonly recurring advice for couples is that they should hold hands often. Human touch has the power to heal mentally, emotionally, and physically. Scientific studies suggest that the simple act of holding hands can stir an instant intimacy, and heighten our awareness and express a deep connection to another person. This mysterious gesture affects the way we think, improves our physical well-being, and notably impacts our emotions.[21] In a small but significant way, holding hands literally has the power to improve your marriage. Consider this, Jesus reaches out with nail-scarred hands to prove the power of his never-ending forgiveness and love. Like Christ, when you hold each other's hands, you send a subtle but endearing and enduring reminder that you're still there and that no matter what you go through, you'll go through it together. As I think back to some of the rough seasons in my own marriage, I can see my wife and I still holding each other's hands. When we hold hands, it's a small sign along the way that things are going to be alright and that we're going to make it. Every time I hold my wife's hand, it's proof that God's Grace has deepened our love and strengthened our commitment to see things through no matter what, and this Grace can do the same for your marriage.

Holding hands is a gentle way to express that you are content with your spouse no matter what is happening in the marriage. Understand however, that contentment doesn't mean there is an absence of conflict. It simply means that you are committed to work through the issues that press against your relationship. There is nothing wrong with wanting to be happy and content in marriage. God intended for marriage to be fulfilling. However, true satisfaction doesn't come from having no struggles. *True happiness happens when couples persevere through trials in order to share in the triumph that follows. Marriages are the strongest when they overcome their struggles together (Romans 8:17).*

The longer you are married, you will eventually encounter significant difficulties, and may even imagine what it would be like to separate. No marriage at any level is always easy. However, if marriage was easy, you wouldn't really need Grace. Embracing God's grace for your marriage is the bonding factor that brings stability and contentment in marriage. Grace never gives up. Grace always endures. Grace is sacrificial, steady, and constant. Grace stays in the fight. Grace has grit. When the struggle is real, Grace is even more real. When your marriage is struggling, don't run from each other; run to Jesus for GRACE!

"Let us then approach God's throne of Grace with confidence, so that we may receive mercy and find Grace to help us in our time of need." (Hebrews 4:16 NIV)

This may be difficult to accept, but sometimes trials in marriage can be helpful in building strong character. Suffering doesn't always have to result in disaster. It can actually have a holy outcome (Romans 5:3-5; 2 Corinthians 4:17-18). Consider that the struggle you are currently facing could actually be a blessing in your marriage. Many couples seek to escape their suffering and will do anything to be *happy*, including divorce. However, running way from suffering may mean skipping a necessary season of growth. Speaking of seasons, marriages go through seasons (Ecclesiastes 3:1-8). Yet, the good news is SEASONS CHANGE! Just because it may be *Fall* or *Winter* in your marriage, and the sun is behind the clouds, doesn't mean the sun isn't there at all. The clouds will pass. God's promises for your marriage are still in motion. Hang in there. Spring is coming!

Struggle in marriage is the crucible where true love is forged—the kiln where our love for one another is purified (Proverbs 17:3). The fiery trials we experience in marriage serve to burn the selfishness out of us. Often, the pain we feel in marriage is simply selfishness dying. When we feel the flames in the furnace of marriage, we must remember that God himself is the refiner. We must learn to trust him. He knows exactly what he is doing. He knows just how to temper our self-centered hearts on the anvil of his Grace. Couples who have made it to their golden years in marriage can tell you they have been through the fire, and then some. However, if you were to ask them, they would probably tell you that the fiery trials they went through proved the genuineness of their steadfast faith in God, attested their love toward one another, and more fully revealed Christ in their marriage.

"So that the tested genuineness of your faith—more precious than gold that perishes though it is tested by fire—may be found to result in praise and glory and honor at the revelation of Jesus Christ." (1 Peter 1:7 NIV)

Many couples make the false assumption that Christian marriage is a bubble from trouble. Quite the contrary. In fact, marriage is often even more susceptible to struggles and pain because of the nature of two people merging into one flesh. Marriage can be pure joy. No earthly pleasure can be compared to it. However, in marriage you will also have the opportunity to learn endurance through suffering. All too often couples refuse to walk through suffering and opt to push the divorce *button*. However, divorce is not necessarily an escape from suffering. In fact, it can be a whole new level of agony for everyone involved. No matter the circumstance, know that God has an endless supply of Grace for your marriage to endure the toughest of times. There is Grace for the grind. Divorce does not have to be the final course!

So, let's continue to discover more about how we can learn to work through the struggles of marriage in our next chapter.

Chapter 11

SKETCH, ETCH AND STRETCH

Thankfully, the Bible addresses tough times in marriage. One such extremely difficult marriage we can learn from is the life of Hosea and Gomer (Hosea 1:2-3:5). Their story starts out with God commanding Hosea to marry Gomer who is currently living as a prostitute.

"When the Lord first spoke through Hosea, the Lord said to Hosea, "Go, take to yourself a wife of whoredom…" (Hosea 1:2 ESV)

I realize this is an extremely severe case. However there is much we can learn about the amazing Grace of God and how we can apply it in our marriages. Ponder this for a moment. When you married your spouse you most likely didn't marry a prostitute or someone with this nature of ill repute. However, you did marry someone with some *ills*. All of us carry a reasonable list of hang-ups, some big and others small. When you marry someone, you inherit their good but also some bad mixed in. You didn't marry the perfect person, you simply married a PERSON that comes with a complex history of emotional, mental, and relational baggage Yet, if you realize early on that the person you married isn't the *ideal* person, it will help you better *deal* with the surprises and shocks along the way and enable you to more successfully process through them. There are three things that happen throughout the course of a Godly marriage. I call it the *sketch*, *etch,* and *stretch* of marriage.

First we have the SKETCH of a marriage. This is the image we conjure up of the picture perfect marriage we've fantasized about all our lives. All too often, couples marry with false expectations of a perfect storyboard sketch of marriage. At first, this idea of marriage looks more like an outlined pencil drawing that is unfilled, uncolored, and missing some important details. Images come to mind of Prince Charming galloping up on a pure white stallion, sweeping the princess off of her feet, and riding out into the sunset of a happily ever after. Of course, this is a make-believe world that comes nowhere even close to reality. Marriage is much more than a page in a coloring book.

Secondly there's the ETCH of a marriage. This is a deeper work in the life of a couple. An etching is where an artist uses a sharpened tool called a *graver* to carve into a metal plate creating a detailed image imbedded into the surface that results in a permanent engraving. When God is *engraving* the masterpiece of marriage, it can be a painful process. God is carving a beautiful image beyond the surface of the marriage to deepen and permeate a couple's love, commitment, and life together. Imagine the pain Hosea felt when Gomer *repeatedly* returned to her old lovers. Yet, God tells Hosea to go after her regardless.

"The LORD said to me, "Go, show your love to your wife again, though she is loved by another man and is an adulteress. Love her as the LORD loves the Israelites, though they turn to other gods…" (Hosea 3:1 NIV)

Hosea had a choice whether to make it work or abandon God's plan altogether. He had every right to be *happy*, but happiness apart from God's plan isn't happiness at all. Hosea's priorities were in order. Like the old hymn says, *"To be happy in Jesus is to trust and obey."* Hosea's love for God was stronger than the struggle. His faith in God was greater than his faith in Gomer. This gave him courage and strength to trust and obey God and persevere in his marriage no matter how hopeless it looked. *The story of Hosea is one of the greatest examples of Christ's unselfish love. He gave up everything to take to himself a broken and sinful bride: you and me (Ephesians 5:25). He totally surrendered his rights to be happy or fulfilled in order to rescue us from a fatal conclusion. Hosea's display of unconditional love is the perfect illustration of what Christ did for us. We were people of the streets, sinful, prostituting our hearts to the world, Yet, Jesus ran after us with an abandon. What a story of amazing love and grace.*

It's important to note here that Gomer's failures are not directed just to wives, nor are Hosea's persistent displays of grace typical to husbands only. We ALL in marriage display characteristics of both Hosea and Gomer. No matter who you more relate to in this story, there is hope for the redemption of your marriage. Whatever side you're on, we no better display God's grace than when we pursue one another regardless of the deep hurt or heartache caused by our spouses. Through Christ, we can do what seems impossible (Matthew 19:26; Philippians 4:13). Marriage problems are NO problem for God!

Thirdly, there's the STRETCH in marriage. It must have been excruciatingly painful for Hosea when God told him to go after Gomer even though she once again returned to her life of prostitution. Can you imagine it? Hosea preaches his heart out during the day and then lies in bed wrestling all through the night. Where is Gomer and what she is doing? His imagination runs wild. Yet, the next day as the sun rises, there he is, searching for her to bring her home. To be honest, this challenges even the furthest limits of where my own love could go. Here is a deeply loving, devoted, dedicated, hardworking, and patient husband, father, and prophet selflessly loving his wayward wife back from the streets where he originally found her. I love how the late author Richard L. Strauss puts it...

> *"So he began his search, driven by that indestructible divine love, love that bears all things, believes all things, hopes all things, endures all things, love that never ends. And he found her, ragged, torn, sick, dirty, disheveled, destitute, chained to an auction block in a filthy slave market, a repulsive shadow of the woman she once was. We wonder how anyone could love her now. But Hosea bought her from her slavery for fifteen shekels of silver and thirteen bushels of barley (Hosea 3:2). Then he said to her, "You shall stay with me for*

197

many days. You shall not play the harlot, nor shall you have a man; so I will also be toward you." (Hosea 3:3) He actually paid for her, brought her home, and eventually restored her to her position as his wife. While we do not find anything else in Scripture about their relationship with each other, we assume that God used Hosea's supreme act of forgiving love to melt her heart and change her life."[5]

Now can you see how Hosea and Gomer's story so vividly portrays a radiant example of Christ's relentless, unwavering, redemptive love, and how it has the prevailing potential to turn any marriage around? Christ pursued us at all costs, and now our covenant with him is permanent. Nothing can tear our hearts away from his Grace. This is an enduring example of how we can give one another grace, especially when our marriage is deeply struggling and even seriously jeopardized. In the *stretch* of marriage, through Christ, we can go far beyond what we are able to bear in our own strength. *Extraordinary marriages don't just happen from what we've learned to DO, but rather from how we've learned to ENDURE.* The Grace of God produces super-elastic love. Scriptures tell us where sin abounds, God's grace even more abounds (Romans 5:20). Grace far exceeds the *lines* of your spouse's failures. In the *stretch* of

198

marriage, when it seems like our faith and patience is being tested to its snapping point, it can drive us to our knees. Yet, it's on our knees that we discover the strength to stand against all odds. *Falling on our knees is the power stance in marriage.* The greatest place of humility is surrender. That's when grace comes rushing in. God resists our pride, but gives us grace in our brokenness (James 4:6).

Sometimes in the *stretch* of marriage, the problem isn't just with your spouse. Have you considered that there may also be unresolved issues in your *own* heart? God doesn't answer prideful prayers. If you keep praying for God to just change your spouse, it will be more difficult for you to see what God may also be doing in you and in the bigger picture of your marriage. Allow God to stretch YOUR faith. Keep praying, believing, trusting, forgiving and looking for the good in your spouse. Ask God for the strength to love your spouse. Love never fails (1 Corinthians 13:8). You're stronger than you think you are. Also, remember that your spouse isn't your enemy. Satan is the enemy. Submit your anger, disappointment, discouragement and resentment to the Lord. By this, you defy the work of the devil and he eventually must flee (James 4:7). The struggle is much deeper than the visible skirmish in your marriage. There is a spiritual war at work here (Ephesians 6:12). Resist the urge to lash out at your spouse. Instead, surrender the fight to God. Be mindful to worship! God hasn't changed. He is still on the throne and completely in control. Worship opens the door for supernatural victories (2 Chronicles 20:20-23). Know that the battle belongs to the Lord, and he never loses a battle (2 Chronicles 20:15). Know that your current struggles are dwarfed by the greater weight of glory God is working out in your behalf (2 Corinthians 4:17). Marital pain has the potential of producing in us great patience and perseverance (Romans 5:3). By patience and perseverance we lay hold of the promises of God (Galatians 6:9; Hebrews 6:12; 10:35; James 5:11). This means God's promises to heal and restore your marriage. *Your marriage will never learn to rise above the flood until it encounters a flood.* The deeper the troubles in your marriage, the deeper God takes you in your faith. Hold on! God hasn't abandoned you or your marriage. You are not alone! Know that God can even use the present pain, confusion, unresolved issues, and seemingly impossible circumstances to accomplish his purposes in your marriage (Romans 8:28).

The pain you are experiencing in your marriage is God working love out in your marriage. He's bringing a greater measure of love out of your heart for one another than you ever thought possible. When you reach out to grab a beautiful rose you will feel the sting of the thorns. This illustrates that with every beautiful marriage comes some pain attached to it. Don't be deceived. Every exemplary marriage has had to endure some significant pain at one time or another. In the stretch of marriage, ask God for the faith to believe that he is enlarging your capacity to love and that your marriage can truly resemble the breadth of his Grace?

Let's be honest, we've all been through our share of marriage struggles. Anyone who's been married for any reasonable amount of time can tell you that marriage difficulties are some of the greatest challenges to navigate. Yet, when a couple refuses to give up and love one another together through thick and thin, they display an enduring faith to the world around them. This is a marriage that has been founded on grace, built by grace, and kept by grace. God wants our marriages to be living examples of His everlasting love and relentless Grace. Grace made marriages stand the test of time.

At the end of the day, working through struggles in marriage is just plain tough, and there is often no two ways around it. It's simply a matter of pushing THROUGH it. *However, just because you may be suffering in your marriage, doesn't mean you should surrender your marriage.* God can turn the battle into a blessing and make sense out of the nonsense. Don't believe the lie that your marriage is impossible and that divorce is the only solution. When you close your heart, you close the doors to all the possibilities. You can't open the heart of your spouse (that's God's job). However, you can open YOUR heart. Ask God to help you let go of any unresolved pride, resentment, anger, or prolonged disappointment you may be harboring. *It's hard to see things clearly through the fog of offence.* When you are honest with God and allow Him to help you work through your own issues, you'll begin to discover the amazing ways that God can redeem and restore your marriage.

Lastly… Don't go it alone! Wholeheartedly seek out Godly wisdom and honest counsel. Do everything in your power to stay together, but more importantly, fully lean on GOD'S power. Don't rely on your own understanding. Know that God is doing a much deeper work beyond the surface (Proverbs 3:5-6). Don't be ashamed to get Christian counseling (I emphasize Christian counseling). We all need help especially when times are desperate. Reach out to those who will tell you the truth of God's Word, not just what you want to hear. Call on trusted pastors and leaders to come alongside you. Lean on the love and support of your church family. That's what they are there for. If you isolate yourself, you go against all wise judgment (Proverbs 18:1). And by all means, don't hang out with and get marriage advice from unhappy and troubled divorcees or those who have become bitter from past broken relationships (Psalms 1:1). *Every marriage is one toxic friendship away from falling apart. Closely guard who you allow into your life.*[16] Instead, look to those, who by God's grace, have successfully navigated through their struggles and have developed a joyful, fruitful and lasting marriage. They will be an incredible source of encouragement and inspiration to you during the difficult times. Do whatever it takes to let God's Grace take over in your marriage. Refuse to use the word *divorce* in your vocabulary. For a couple committed to a Grace made marriage, there is ALWAYS hope!

Chapter 12

WEATHERING THE STORMS

Grace is what you are going to need to weather the storms in your marriage. I call it *Cleaving Grace*. Cleaving will keep you from leaving. Cleaving is the security and the anchor of a marriage. Cleaving to one another in the time of storms is the only way your marriage will make it. Cleaving in marriage is like a cement foundation. It is what the entire house stands on. If there are cracks in the foundation, the house will not make it when the storms come and the ground shifts.

When you leave your parents and enter marriage you are to cleave to your mate (Genesis 2:24). The Hebrew word for cleave is *dabaq* (daw-bach) which means to catch by pursuit, follow hard after, and overtake. To cleave is to be pervasively active. It is a continuous, relentless pursuing of another person. It has the attitude that says, *"If you ever leave me, I'll just have to go with you."* Miram Webster's Dictionary defines *cleave* as "a sticking together of parts so that they form a unified mass." Cleaving is much more than just holding onto; it's molding into. It has the connotation of two separate and uniquely different elements merging or molding into one element (i.e. water and dirt becoming mud). When we are saved we are inseparably and eternally bonded to Christ (1 Corinthians 1:17). We literally become one with him. Likewise, when you are married you are eternally and inseparably amalgamated. Cleave doesn't just mean to *tie the knot*. Tying the knot implies that it can be untied. It is in this way that couples must relentlessly cleave to one another when the hurricane winds are swirling around them. If you don't already know this, the storms are coming. You may be in sunny days now, but there are clouds forming in the distance. However, you don't have to fear. Although love won't redirect the storm, love will give you direction through the storm. *Love can't change the weather, but through love, you can weather the changes.* Love is the gravity that keeps the storms from tearing your marriage apart.

Remember, you're living life together and so you're going to experience all that comes with it together. Just don't forget each other when the storms come. You're a team. A team that wins stays in the fight. It's easy to get self-focused when troubles arise but remember, you're in it together and you can better weather the storms together (Ecclesiastes 4:9-12). Many times neither of you will be to blame for the storms. Things will be totally out of your control. Although you can't control the storm around your marriage, you don't have to let the storm control your marriage. When there is nothing you can do, hold tightly to one another and keep your eyes on Jesus.

"…We do not know what to do, but our eyes are on You." (2 Chronicles 20:12b NASB)

My parents recently celebrated their golden wedding anniversary. To be sure, they've had struggles just like any other marriage. Yet, here they are, 50 years later, and still in love. They've navigated through almost everything imaginable: babies, toddlers, teenage catastrophes, financial difficulties, the change of life, college debt, heart surgery, retirement, and so much more. Yet, they cleaved to each other until the storms left! They survived! They've weathered every storm!

I've learned interesting things about weathering storms through a recent study of grizzly bears. Grizzlies have the innate ability to survive the harshest of winters. Grizzly bears need food to survive and during the winter food is scarce. If they don't hibernate, chances are they will starve and die. To prepare for hibernation, grizzlies eat more than usual during the Fall to store up extra body fat. During hibernation they will use up this extra body fat to live off of while not losing any muscle. When grizzlies eventually drop into deep sleep their body temperature plummets so much that it actually matches the outside temperature. Also, a grizzly's pulse and rate of breathing slows down so significantly that they will not wake up by loud noises or even if they are moved or touched.[18] Grizzly bears survive the storms by burying themselves in their caves and simply waiting it out. Grace in marriage is like two grizzly bears hibernating peacefully together while the blizzard is howling outside. They don't stress, they rest in the peace of God (Colossians 3:15). They bear down, bear under, bear up and bear through everything life throws at their marriage; and when the spring comes, they bound up stronger and more powerful than before the winter season began.

Scripture tells us that when you walk through deep waters and the enemy crashes down like a tidal wave against your marriage, the Lord himself will be embankment around you to keep the floods at bay (Isaiah 59:19). When the storms come, that's the time to batten down the hatches, grab onto one another and lean in tight. The way to survive in a disaster is to take shelter together. As you cleave to one another, Jesus stands between your marriage and the storms.

I want to share some final thoughts that will help you as you weather the storms that come against your marriage. These are not 10 Commandments for a great marriage. Rules don't make a marriage. Relationship makes a marriage. Rather, these should be considered as safeguards, or rather I prefer to call them GRACE-guards, that will help shape a mindset and heart attitude as you continue the journey towards a fulfilling and long lasting marriage. "Grace-guards" imply that you are committed to cherish and preserve the heart of Grace in your relationship; that it will be the governing theme of your marriage. You could even think of these as ways to storm-proof your marriage, just like you would prepare for a storm coming toward your home.

1. Close the Door.

This may seem obvious, but to many it is not. When the weather is bad outside, you don't leave the door open. You close the door and even lock it. Don't let the storm inside your home. If things are terrible around you (i.e. politics, world affairs, friend's marriages failing, extended family drama, problems on the job, complications with children, etc.) Don't let it into the protective circle around your marriage. Jesus said we would be pressed about on the outside but not shaken (2 Corinthians 4:8-9). Why? Because we refuse to let every other drama into our marriage. Closing the door also means the past is over. Quit rehashing the past. No matter what happened, close the door to the past. The only way you can move forward is to forget what's behind you.

2. Adjust the Thermostat.

Sometimes when it's cold you just have to turn up the heat. Passion is the heat in marriage. Passion often wanes because of the pace of life, kids, job, responsibilities, etc. When was the last time you had fulfilling connection? Sometimes just making the decision to come together in conversation and sexual intimacy can greatly help the marriage. The first thing a woman cannot do without is affection and the second thing is attentive conversation. The first thing a man cannot do without is sexual fulfillment. The second is sexual fulfillment, and the third is sexual fulfillment... Seriously though, for a woman emotional connection, conversation, and attention fuels sexual intimacy. A woman is like a cell phone. She likes to be held and talked to, but if you push the wrong button, you will be disconnected. For a man, affirmation and physical attraction fuels sexual intimacy. Contrary to popular belief, if a man feels demeaned by his wife and has a lack of affirmation, then his sexual connection can be lost. In short, a man and woman are different but the truth is they both rate emotional connection and sexual fulfillment high on the scale. Sometimes when things aren't going well in the marriage it can be simply due to a lack of planned connection, both emotionally and physically. Purposely creating moments for intimacy is a way to turn up the heat in the marriage. Men should plan for moments of deep conversation and undivided attention for their wives. As well, wives should look for ways to affirm their husbands. If men and women devote themselves to giving to the other in these areas, sexual fulfillment will often be naturally unhindered. Of course, this subject is much more complex in nature. A great book I suggest on this topic is "His Needs, Her needs (Building an Affair-Proof marriage)" by Willard F. Harley Jr.

3. Open the Vents.

When the bitter chill of winter is imminent or a blizzard is approaching, it's time to turn up the heat and open up the vents. To ensure proper air circulation and heat dispersion throughout the home, the vents must be cleared of soot. Communication is the airflow of a marriage. What is being *aired* out in your marriage? Communication in marriage is like opening the vents. Notice, I didn't say communication is *venting*. There is a difference. What would marriage be like if we didn't just talk to each other? Talking it out keeps things *above ground*. Communication prevents feelings of neglect and resentment from festering. Silence is mystery and when there's mystery, nobody knows how the other feels or what they're thinking. Husbands, if your wife looks attractive in a certain outfit, tell her. Don't just wait until sex to compliment her or she may feel used or treated as a sex object. Wives, if your husband does something nice, don't remind him of all the other times he didn't do something nice. Tell him how much you appreciate it when he is helpful, considerate, and caring. *It is better to regularly open the vents than to vent that which has not been regularly opened.* When couples hold in the good, they tend to also hold in the bad. Too many pent and vent. Venting can be detrimental as it usually is done after a long period of frustrated silence. Time spent in healthy conversation keeps things out in the open. Some couples only choose to talk about the serious issues. However, if you only talk about the serious issues of your marriage, money, kids, work, life, etc., you may tend to avoid communication altogether. A good rule of thumb to remember: if you spend more time talking about positive things in your marriage it will make the not-so-positive subjects easier to discuss. Just talk about everything. My wife and I have an ongoing agreement that there should be no secrets between us (no matter how difficult they are to share).

Also, husbands and wives need to develop skills for conflict resolution. *In matters of resolving conflict, remember to talk to your mate not at them.* You'll get so much farther in conversations and discussions when you practice this one small piece of advice. Although some behaviors in your spouse may mimic that of a child at times, they are not your child, nor should they be spoken to as such. Humility and respect go a long way.[17] Here are a few points to remember when attempting to resolve conflict.[7]

1. Avoid verbal hostility and passive-aggressive language. When sharing concerns, don't attack one another. Rather, learn to express how the other's actions make you feel. When you attack your spouse (although their behavior may seem to warrant it) you actually put them on the defense and they may react undesirably. In resolving conflict it is better to communicate how your emotions are affected, negatively or positively. By this, you create a better chance for your mate to listen than to lash out.[7]

2. Learn to stay in the present and don't dredge up old issues from the past. Ask for what you need, say no to what you can't do, and be open to negotiation and compromise. Articulate a complaint about a specific behavior and express your feelings in a way that is clear, direct and appropriate.[7]

3. Whenever possible, communicate directly with your spouse in person or over the phone versus email or text battles where misunderstandings breed quickly. Where possible, use "I" statements

rather than "you" to reduce defensiveness. For example, *"I am upset that you didn't get my car serviced,"* rather than, *"You are a jerk for forgetting to take care of my car."* Give your spouse time to express what they are feeling. Remember, passion isn't just demonstrated in sexual intimacy. It is also expressed in heated discussion. Try to see resolving conflict in a positive light—like passion working its way into every area of your marriage.[7]

4. Listen and really hear your mate. Ask questions to gather information that will be clarifying but even more importantly listen to their heart. Consider their perspectives or solutions. Look for the compromise or "win-win."[7]

4. Seal the Windows.

When you winterize your house, you put proper seals around the windows to keep heat from escaping and cold air from seeping through. The eyes are the window to the soul. Batten down the hatches and pull the shades for any other person outside your marriage. Jesus said, the eyes are windows that allow the light entrance into our body, mind, and soul (Matthew 6:22-23). While windows let in light, we can also peer out into the darkness through those same windows. We should open the windows to the light but seal them from the darkness. *Keep your eyes off of anyone that tempts you for desires of intimacy.* There's nothing wrong with thinking someone is attractive. However, the second look is the clincher. Here are some things to think about regarding having eyes only for your mate.

1. Don't look into the eyes of another man/woman for too long. Also, let your eyes bounce off of the opposite sex quickly. A lingering look is the hook. Men, keep your eyes off of anything that bounces. Need I say more.

2. Don't be alone with the opposite sex for any significant amount of time and if possible avoid it all together. If you find yourself in this situation, try to leave quickly and then share it with your spouse later on, so nothing remains undisclosed.

3. Don't share your emotional issues with the opposite sex. Women are typically more tempted to be drawn into relationships by emotion. Men know this and will use it to their advantage. A lion is cunning when stalking it's prey.

4. Keep all sexually suggestive and explicit material out of the home and out of your life. Let your spouse have full access to your passwords and login information for all your social media accounts. Maryland and D.C. divorce attorney Regina Demeo says at least 20 percent of her cases involve illicit relationships that began on

Facebook. The stats don't lie. Attorneys estimate that 80 percent of their cases now involve using evidence from Facebook for use in court.[19]

5. Don't entertain sexual thoughts outside of the marriage relationship. By all means, imagine freely about your spouse all the time. Let these words ring true, *"I Only Have Eyes for You."*

5. Fill the Pantry.

It's too late to make a run to the grocery store when the blizzard hits. Your marriage will go through some harsh winter seasons. However, if you invest plenty of time, attention, communication, intimacy, romance, affirmation, service, and appreciation into your mate, when hard times come, you won't feel barren in your marriage (Proverbs 6:6-8). Sometimes prolonged sickness, bad news, drama on the job, extended family issues, trouble with teenagers, etc., are like snow drifts at the front door. However, if you've made generous provisions emotionally, physically, and spiritually into the life of your spouse, it will make going through the winter storms of your marriage much easier. You can survive the brutal winters of marriage if you remember to make provisions in the summer. *Summer love prepares your marriage for the winter lull.*

6. Take Shelter Quickly.

Disaster preparedness is key in surviving major catastrophes. There's no guarantee that disaster won't hit your marriage. It could be in the form of a family death, sudden loss of a job, destruction of the home, ministry transition, major car accident, and the list goes on. These major life happenings can seriously threaten the stability of marriage. Some couples are not spiritually or emotionally equipped to handle major life issues such as these. I've witnessed firsthand a young marriage fall apart when a husband was fired from his job and another marriage split after their young child's death. They didn't make it because they allowed hurt and bitterness to drive them away from God and abandon the church, and attempt to make it on their own. This is common for so many marriages. Couples don't make it because they don't take shelter with God first. In these cases it was devastating to watch. Their dilemma could have been diverted if they would have run quickly to God. Some blame the church for not reaching out, and in some cases the church should take better initiative to minister to these cases. However, it isn't always the church's fault. The church does miss ministry opportunities, but couples struggling in marriage should seek out help from God and the church first. Running away from shelter is not wise when the storm is coming. A friend of mine recently divorced. It was not pretty. Their children were caught in the aftermath and the whole family is still struggling to make sense of it all. The marriage may have survived if he would have come to the church at the onset of his marital difficulties. Don't try to survive alone. God is there for you. He is a refuge in the time of storm, a strong tower from the enemy. Run to him, the church, and trusted pastors and counselors to find safety and solutions for your marriage (Proverbs 18:10).

7. Build a Fire.

A marriage that prays together stays together. Prayer and worship are the logs in the fire place. When it's cold, stoke the fire of prayer, praise and worship. It's interesting that many times my wife and I have felt a great sense of peace when we joined hands and prayed late in the night right before we go to sleep. Often when my wife and I pray together for our home, ministry, children, finances, and more, God helps us make an instant emotional and spiritual connection. Prayer invites the Grace of God to do what only he can do in the marriage. Don't avoid praying together. You don't have to pray long intense prayers, just take regular moments to pray together. Don't be legalistic about it. It doesn't have to be the same time everyday. Just make sure you are doing it. When you pray together, *don't tell God that you have big problems in your marriage; tell the problems in your marriage that you have a BIG God.* This also applies when there is strife between you and your mate. When there is a dispute between me and my wife, I will often pull away to an empty room, get down on my knees and ask God to help us. It's in these moments that I have been able to let go of my pride and invite God to resolve the tension, argument, division, and strife. The only prayers God doesn't answer are the ones we don't pray. Remember, prideful prayers will always fall on deaf ears. Once I am able to see my fault in the matter, I then have power to rebuke the enemy, declare peace, humble myself, and apologize to my wife. It's amazing when I pray how God also moves upon my wife. She's already moving toward me after I pray. *If the fires of prayer and worship are burning, it will make ashes of the issues.* Stop debating the inner voice of the Holy Spirit to allow prayer into your marriage. Fill Your home with it. Grace surfs on the waves of prayer.

8. Get the Forecast.

During the winter of 2014, a major ice storm suddenly hit Atlanta leaving thousands of cars stranded overnight on Interstate highways and multitudes of kids were trapped in schools unable to go home well into the next day. It was absolute pandemonium. Some went without food and water and even ran out of gas on major thoroughfares. The reason this happened is because many Atlanta area businesses and school districts ignored the forecasters report of the coming storm. I even saw Al Roker on the Today show make the report himself. In the past, our school system has often ignored clear reports of snow in our area and has kept kids in school. Of course, we handle snow differently in the south than our friends in the north and mid western states. We're actually wimps in the wintertime. The point I'm making here is *if you don't know the forecast you won't prepare for the storm in time.* This is where this book and so many others on marriage come in. You should take full advantage of all marriage resources out there. Don't think you know everything about marriage. Husbands listen; if your wife asks you to go to a marriage conference, by all means go, especially if it's at a resort away from home and the kids. If you're wife asks you to get away to a place where there is help for your marriage or just to have a refreshing time for you marriage, get there. There will be some surprises waiting there for you in more ways than one. Marriage resources will help you forecast and navigate the many issues that will arise in your marriage. This book is a product of the many books I've read, sermons I've heard, and conferences I've attended on marriage. Marriage resources help you to prepare and invest in your marriage for the stormy times. Nothing but good can come from going to a marriage retreat or reading a book on marriage. We all need special moments in our marriage that offer help. If your church offers a marriage conference or if you can get to a marriage retreat somewhere, then go! Every time my wife and I have gone to a marriage conference our relationship has been refreshed by the information and inspiration we have received.

9. Stock Emergency Supplies.

Weather preparedness agencies instruct us to carry extra blankets and a first aid kid in our cars in the event we are traveling and find ourselves stranded in a storm. As we journey on the road of marriage, storms may suddenly come. First aid is going to God first. Earlier I pointed out that couples should take shelter in a community of faith early, regularly and at first sign of trouble in the marriage. However, going to GOD first is different. Running to God first means having a strong faith in God should not be an option in your marriage. He is our FIRST aid. So many turn to talk shows, gossip magazines, and even worse, other hurt and wounded people. When we have problems in marriage, we must turn to God first. He is our first line of defense. Also, the word of God is a vital part of our first-aid kit. The word of God is the remedy for everything (Proverbs 4:20-22). Fill your marriage and your home with the Word of God. Take time to read the Word separately and as a couple. One word from God can change everything about your marriage. It has the answers so many marriages are desperately seeking. Don't *underestimate* the importance of God's word. You might find yourself too *overwhelmed* to handle the storms.

Also, extra blankets are a necessity for winter preparedness. Who is your covering? Who do you look to for answers? Again, couples should first turn to trusted leaders, licensed counselors, and those who believe and want the best for them and will lovingly speak truth into their lives. Don't avoid spiritual covering for your family. Church relationships and spiritual authority were given to us for our protection. Don't keep your marriage out in the cold. Come under true spiritual authority.

10. Wait it Out.

Many places around the world have storm seasons; times when the weather is very unpredictable and often violent. Monsoon, typhoon, and hurricane season is common to many tropical and coastal regions. There are times in marriage, particularly during career changes, ministry transition, child birth, raising toddlers, both parents working, children leaving home for college, retirement, and the senior years to name a few, that create the potential for storm seasons. Major storms come along with the territory of marriage. There are also times in the marriage that you will struggle for no apparent reason and won't be able to pinpoint the emotional issues. Menopause is a huge season of transition in life for women that can strain the marriage. Now, before the men resort to finger pointing, be aware that menopause isn't just isolated to women. Why do you think they call it MENopause? Some say most of women's problems start with men (i.e.

MENopause, MENtal illness, MENstruation, HISterectomy). This is humorous, but there is some truth to this. There is actually a time in a man's life, usually around his 50's, when things start to break down (i.e. loss of testosterone, loss of memory, sexual dysfunction, insecurity stemming from what used to be and what lies ahead, etc.). Yet, all seasons of marriage are passing seasons. There are seasons of sun and season of rain. However, no matter the season, if you are committed to love each other, believe in one another, and stay open and obedient to God's guidance, your marriage will weather every season. All marriages experience storms, but storms eventually end. Sometimes all we can do is hunker down, wait it out, and trust in God through it all.

"Don't be impatient. Wait for the Lord, and he will come and save you! Be brave, stouthearted, and courageous. Yes, wait and he will help you." (Psalms 27:13-14 TLB)

You can use this verse as you pray for your marriage. Put the words "our marriage" in place of the word "you" and read it aloud. If Jesus is Lord of your marriage, you are in great shape to weather the storms. If Jesus is not the Lord of your marriage, let him in right now. He is standing at the door, knocking, asking you to let him into your relationship (Revelation 3:20). In today's world the statistics are pretty low of your marriage surviving without Jesus at the center. Jesus is the saving Grace for your marriage.

A death storm came to the Egyptians and God told the Israelites to paint lamb's blood on the doorposts of their homes and the death cloud passed over them. Jesus is our Passover lamb (Hebrews 11:28). Likewise, when you surrender your marriage to Jesus and accept him as Savior and Lord of your future, the survival rate of your marriage immediately begins to rise. The Grace of God will put your marriage up-and-over. Are you ready to make Jesus the center or your marriage? Just like you once prayed the prayer for salvation, you can pray a salvation prayer for your marriage. Let God's amazing Grace sweep into your marriage. If you are with your mate right now, join hands and pray this. If you are alone pray it all the same. Everything is about to change for you. I can feel it. Pray this prayer...

Heavenly father, we believe right now that our marriage is at the threshold of a brand-new dawn. Daybreak has come! We believe with all our hearts that you are the Son of God and the Lord of our marriage. Where there is darkness, bring light. Where there is hatred, bring love. Where there is unforgiveness and bitterness, help us to let it all go. Forgive us for not allowing you to be the center of our marriage. Cleanse us from all resentment and accusation against one another. We surrender our pride and arrogance and admit where we are wrong. We repent for times we have hurt, neglected, or belittled one another. We are moving forward in your Grace.

We are truly thankful for one another. We accept each other as your special gift in our lives. We are a perfect fit for each other and we will believe nothing less. We were made for each other. We will not give up on each other.

We will seek out help and join ourselves to loving family, Godly counsel, trusted advisors, and honest friendships to help us weather the difficult storms of our marriage. Renew within us a passionate love for one another. Remove all regret. It's not what we did or haven't done in our marriage, but it's what YOU have already done in our marriage and what you are about to do. We have great expectations because you are a great God. It's a new day and there are new mercies unfolding. Help us see each other in a new light… YOUR light!

Right now we avow our steadfast love for one another. Revive our trust in you. Help us to do what we can in the difficult times and give us courage to wait when there's nothing we can do. When the fight calls and we feel too weak to wage war, remind us that the battle for our marriage is yours. You are strong in us and fight for us. Renew within us the desire to walk out the promises we made to one another the day we were first wed. We want to live in your promises. We cannot do this in our own strength. We need you.

We don't want our marriage to be what it used to be. We want our marriage to be all you want it to be. Greater days are ahead. Lead us into the bright future that you have planned for us. We rest on the promise that you will never give up on our marriage. Come fill our marriage with your Grace. Make our marriage everything it was meant to be. And because your Grace is so extraordinary, our marriage will be anything but ordinary. Ours is a marriage made by your love... a Grace made marriage!

Amen!

Chapter 13

PROMISES FOR MARRIAGE

This final chapter should not only be read but also be used for prayer and proclamation. My wife and I are firm believers in prayer and the confession of God's Word over every area of our lives. The Word of God has helped us through many difficult times as a couple. We've confessed and prayed the promises of God more times than we can remember. So anywhere we have found the Grace of God in scripture, we have held on tightly to it and seen God do the miraculous in our marriage. All the promises of God are for your marriage too, and they are totally affirmed in his Word and accessed by faith through His Grace. I highly recommend that you take full advantage of these Grace-filled passages in the next few pages.

"For no matter how many promises God has made, they are "Yes" in Christ. And so through him the "Amen" is spoken by us to the glory of God." (1 Corinthians 1:20 NIV)

Grace is the unmerited favor of God, and that favor is not contingent upon your behavior but upon the Savior. God loves your marriage, not because either one of you are lovable, but because he is love. His Grace for your marriage is not based upon your performance but a PERSON and a PROMISE. The following scripture promises have been repurposed and rephrased into powerful prayers and proclamations that you can use as mighty confessions as you and your mate boldly pray them together. The integrity of each verse has been fully preserved to directly apply to your marriage. Stand firmly on these promises. Pray them aloud together and let the Holy Spirit guide you as you pray and believe them accordingly. You will be amazed at the doors that will open as you stand together in prayer and agreement for your marriage. There is no force equal to a couple who faithfully prays for their marriage. No matter how big the mountain, it is no match for God's Grace. (Zechariah 4:7)

God is the originator of your marriage. Your marriage was conceived by him. Your marriage is no accident or happenstance. Because of this, the Holy Spirit will be a constant companion to your marriage. He will never abandon you. He will defend your marriage. He will be by you, with you and, for you until death do you part, until time is no more.

MARRIAGE PROMISES

Our marriage is God's divine help for the both of us. We are far better together than we are separate and alone. We need each other, and we are *Godsends* to one another. (Genesis 2:18)

God will exceedingly multiply us in every area of our marriage. He will indeed greatly bless our marriage, and our children shall overcome all barriers in their lives because of the example our marriage sets for them. (Genesis 17:2; 22:17)

God places a shield around our marriage and wards off imposters, intruders and invaders. He throws any attempts of infidelity into confusion. All those who plot to come against our marriage utterly fail. God has made all enemies, schemers, and third parties against our marriage quickly scatter from us. (Exodus 23:27 NASB)

We will not be afraid for our marriage; God will provide for our every need. (Genesis 50:21)

The LORD will fight for our marriage, and we will hold our peace. (Exodus 14:14)

God has sent an angel before our marriage to guard it along the way and to bring us into the place which he has prepared for us. (Exodus 23:20)

God will provide rain in the dry times of our marriage, and we will be fruitful in every season regardless of circumstances. All the Grace we allow into our marriage will cause us to naturally yield the fruit of love, devotion, passion, and service to one another. (Leviticus 32:34)

The LORD himself goes before our marriage. He is constantly with us. He will never leave us or forsake us. We will not be afraid or discouraged. (Deuteronomy 31:8)

The LORD will open the heavens, the full storehouse of his bounty, and send rain on our marriage and will bless all the work of our hands. In turn, we will be a shining example to many marriages. We will have more than enough to bless others. (Deuteronomy 28:12)

The Lord will causes our marriage to prosper in every way. (Deuteronomy 30:9)

The eternal God is a dwelling place for our marriage. Our marriage is in his everlasting arms. He drives out all quarreling, discouragement, and defeat from our relationship. (Deuteronomy 33:27)

God is the refuge and rock of our marriage. He is the shield and stronghold of our love, affection, and devotion. He has saved our marriage from the violence of the enemy. Because of his Grace, our marriage is indestructible. (2 Samuel 22:3)

For the eyes of the LORD move to and fro throughout the earth that He may strongly support our marriage because our hearts are completely His. (2 Chronicles 16:9)

We will not fear or be dismayed. The battle for our marriage belongs to the Lord. God is fighting for our marriage. We will see the salvation of the LORD on our behalf. The LORD himself is with us. (Chronicles 20:15-17)

The God of Heaven will give our marriage success as we building our relationship on the foundation of Grace. (Nehemiah 2:20)

Though our earlier days seemed great, our marriage is better than ever. Our greatest days are ahead of us. The best is yet to come! (Job 8:7)

You, O LORD, are a shield around our marriage. Our marriage reflects your glory. You graciously lift our heads. All our enemies will turn back from attacking our marriage and they will suddenly be ashamed. (Psalms 3:3-7)

You have blessed our marriage and made us righteous by your Grace. You surround our marriage with favor like a shield. (Psalms 5:12)

Because of your endless Grace, we completely trust in you for our marriage. You have never forsaken the couple who seeks you. (Psalms 9:10)

God is the inheritance for our marriage, our cup of blessing never stops overflowing. You guard all that is ours. We know the LORD is always with us. We will not be shaken. (Psalms 16:5-8)

The LORD is our rock and our fortress and our deliverer, our God, our rock, in whom we take refuge; our shield and the strength and salvation, of our marriage. (Psalms 18:2)

God, you deliver our marriage from our enemies; and lift us above those who rise up against us;

You rescue us from the deceiving schemers. (Psalms 18:48)

God, you will send our marriage help directly from the sanctuary of your Heaven. (Psalms 20:2)

The LORD is the light and salvation of our marriage. God saves our marriage. We will not fear, The LORD is the defense of our marriage; There is no dread. When evil comes upon our marriage to devour it, our adversaries and our enemies will stumble and fall. Though a host encamp against our marriage, our heart will not fear; Though war arise against our marriage, in spite of this we shall be confident... For in the day of trouble, God will conceal us in His tabernacle; In the secret place of His tent, He will hide us; He will lift us up on a rock. And now, our head will be lifted up above the enemies of our marriage. We will offer praise with shouts of joy; we will sing, yes, we will sing praises to the LORD. (Psalms 27:1-6)

O LORD, by Your favor You have made our marriage to stand strong. You delight in the prosperity of our marriage. The integrity of our marriage is strong enough to withstand any storm because we are in Your presence forever. (Psalms 41:12; 30:7; 35:27)

You have saved our marriage from our adversaries, and You have put to shame those who hate us. (Psalms 44:7)

The favor of the Lord our God is upon our marriage and you confirm the work of our hands. (Psalms 90:17)

Our marriage is at peace in God's presence. He is our refuge. We trust in you and we are safe. That's right, you rescue our marriage from hidden traps and from all deadly hazards. Your huge outstretched arms protect us; under them we are perfectly safe; your arms fend off all harm. No fear at night, no anxiety in the day, no dread that prowls through the darkness, no disaster that suddenly hits will shake us. Even though other marriages are falling and failing all around us, no harm will even graze ours. We will stand untouched. Yes, because God is our refuge, the Most High God of our home, evil can't get close to us. Harm can't get through the door. God has ordered his angels to guard our marriage wherever we go. If we stumble, we won't panic because you'll catch us; you'll keep us from failing and falling. We'll walk unharmed among lions and snakes, and kick young lions and serpents from the path of our marriage. (Psalms 91:1-15)

For God has shattered bronze gates and broken bars of iron that have bound our marriage. Every door is opening! The LORD will give us increase for every lack. (Psalms 107:15-16; 115:14)

The LORD keeps watch over our marriage as we come and go, both now and forever. (Psalms 121:8)

Peace is within the walls of our marriage, family and home. Prosperity is within all our dwelling places. (Psalms 122:7)

The Lord will perfect all that concerns our marriage. (Psalms 138:8)

God creates peace in our marriage; He satisfies us with the best of everything. (Psalms 147:14)

Our marriage has a good reputation. We trust you with all our heart for our marriage. We do not lean on our own understanding. We commit all the dealings of our marriage to You. You will make our marriage firm, strong and straight. (Proverbs 3:4-6)

Our bodies will glow with health, our very bones will vibrate with life. We will never stop having great chemistry in our sexual intimacy. Our physical relationship honors God. Our times in our bedroom will burst and run over with true happiness and joy. (Proverbs 3:7-10)

(Husbands confess) I have found an amazing wife. She is God's favor in my life. (Proverbs 18:22)

We are better together. We will have an enduring reward for our love. When we fall we will be there for each other. Our love will warm us because we are together. If outside forces threaten to negatively influence or overpower our marriage, we will not be cast down . We have the power to resist infidelity and intruders into our marriage. Our strand of love cannot be broken. (Ecclesiastes 4:9-12)

When our marriage passes through deep waters, God is with us; we will not drown. The current will not take us under. When we walk through the fire we will not be burned, nor be scorched by the flames. We are fireproof! (Isaiah 43:2)

God energizes our marriage when we get weary and gives fresh strength to continue the journey. Our marriage will be stronger than when we were married in our youth. Even in old age our relationship soars. (Isaiah 49:29-31)

God's love surrounds us. Thus, our love for each other grows stronger everyday. (Isaiah 52:12-13)

We will not allow humiliation to taint our marriage. Our integrity will stand strong and we will not be disgraced. (Isaiah 54:4)

No weapon created and turned against our marriage will succeed. We will not accuse each other. God will vindicate any attack made by the enemy on our marriage. Satan will not succeed in his attempts to break us apart. (Isaiah 54:17)

Instead of shame in our marriage, we will have a double portion of Grace. Instead of humiliation, we will have everlasting joy. (Isaiah 61:7)

Our marriage is like a strong tree planted by the water, that extends its roots by a stream and will not droop when the heat comes. It's leaves will flourish. We will not fear when other marriages are experiencing drought. We will not cease to bear fruit. (Jeremiah 17:8)

God will satisfy our relationship and refresh us when love languishes. The Holy Spirit is fostering an atmosphere of peace in our home creating an atmosphere for a healthy marriage. (Jeremiah 31:25; 33:6)

God has given our marriage a good name, and a solid reputation of distinction among all the other marriages around us. When there is loss in our marriage, he will restore our fortunes before our very eyes and the eyes of others. (Zephaniah 3:20)

We are one in our marriage. Undivided! Although we have differences and disagreements, God has joined us together with by a force that cannot be divided or dissolved. (Matthew 19:4-6)

We receive all we ask for in our marriage in Jesus name; and it brings glory to Jesus. (John 14:13-14)

The Holy Spirit defends our marriage. He is our Advocate. The Holy Spirit teaches us to have a great marriage and we respond to all we are learning. There is peace in our marriage. Therefore, we will not let our hearts be troubled or afraid. (John 14:26-27)

God is the source of our marriage, the vine. We are the branches coming from that vine. As we trust in him, his life will surge through our marriage, and we will be fruitful. (John 15:5-6)

God will abundantly protect and provide for our marriage in the name of Jesus. We freely receive all he has for us with abundant joy. (John 16:24)

We receive an abundance of Grace and the gift of righteousness for our marriage. Thereby, we will reign in life through Jesus Christ. (Romans 5:17)

God is filling our marriage with joy and peace. Our marriage is abounding in hope by the power of the Holy Spirit. (Romans 15:13)

Our love for one another believes all things, hopes all things and endures all things. There is nothing that we cannot overcome. (1 Corinthians 13:7)

We thank God for comforting us in all our marriage struggles. We know that the momentary troubles in our marriage are nothing compared to all God is doing for us. Everything God is preparing for us far outweighs all our struggles. (2 Corinthians 1:3-4; 4:17)

God's Grace abounds in our marriage. It is more than enough for everything we need and encounter. (2 Corinthians 9:8)

Jesus loves our marriage. He gave his life for our marriage. He is cleansing our marriage with his word, his spirit, and his love. Jesus makes us radiant, without stains, free from wrinkles or any blemishes. Our marriage is holy and blameless in his Grace. (Ephesians 5:25-27)

Our marriage can endure all things through Christ who strengthens us. God will supply all we need in our marriage according to His riches in glory by Christ Jesus. God was faithful to join us together, and he will keep us together by that same faithfulness. (Philippians 4:13; 1 Thessalonians 5:24)

The Lord is faithful. He will strengthen and protect our marriage from the evil one. He will never abandon or forsake our marriage. (2 Thessalonians 3:3; Hebrews 13:5-6)

We will never lack wisdom and insight for our marriage. All we have to do is ask God for what we need, and he will give it to us without holding anything back. (James 1:5)

Our prayers are unhindered because we give Grace, understanding, and honor to one another. We will not sow dishonor in our marriage. (1 Peter 3:7)

Though we experience seasons of suffering in our marriage, the God of all Grace, who called us together to experience His eternal glory in Christ, will Himself perfect, confirm, strengthen, and establish us. (1 Peter 5:10)

Our marriage will prosper and be in health in all aspects. By God's Grace every conflict in our relationship is being resolved. (John 1:2)

ABOUT THE AUTHOR

For nearly three decades, Tony Sutherland has served on staff in the local church as well as traveled extensively around the world, stirring in hearts everywhere a passion for Jesus and a powerful Grace awakening through his music, teaching, and preaching. Tony has captured the unique ability to effectively reach a wide diversity of people in the church. His dynamic ministry style crosses denominational and cultural barriers, impacting people of every age. Along with his busy traveling schedule, Tony has served on staff as a Worship Leader at Free Chapel in Gainesville, GA under the ministry of Pastor Jentezen Franklin for the past 12 years.

Tony is also an accomplished songwriter having written songs for artists such as Israel Houghton, Ricardo Sanchez, CeCe Winans, The Katinas, Mandisa, Phillips-Craig & Dean, Bishop Paul Morton, William Murphy, David & Nichole Binion, Ashmont Hill, Daryl Coley, Myron Butler, Ron Kenoly and many others.

Tony resides in the North Atlanta area with his beautiful wife Sherri of 27 years and their two amazing children, Anna (15) and Asher (20).

ENDNOTES

1. "Three Ways to Love Your Imperfect Husband." by Kim Cash Tate, 2015, www.desiringgod.org.

2. "Marriage and One Way Love." by Tullian Tchvidjian, 2013. www.thinke.org.

3. "Grace Works." by Tony Sutherland, Tony Sutherland Ministries, Inc., 2010, www.tonysutherland.com.

4. "The Meaning of Marriage." (page 19) by Tim Keller with Kathy Keller, Riverhead Books, The Penguin Group, 375 Hudson St., New York, NY, 10014, 2011.

5. "Undying Love-The Story of Hosea and Gomer." by Richard L. Strauss, 2004, www.bible.org. Reprinted with permission.

6. "Staying Together (The Politically Incorrect Guide)." By Rick Creasy, Deeper Revelation Books, P.O. Box 4260, Cleveland, TN 37320, 2014.

7. Adapted from "Ten Tips for Resolving Conflict." by Joyce Marter, LCPC, 2014, www.huffingtonpost.com.

8. "Divorce as an Acronym." by Jackie Walker, 2010, www.thedivorcecoach.wordpress.com.

9. "The Fountain of Forgiveness." by Dr. Karen Gushta, 2013. www.cnsnews.com.

10. "Women Need More Sleep Than Men Because of Their 'Complex' Brains, Research Suggests." by Will Worley, 2016, www.independent.co.uk.

11. How Do Respondents Answer Survey Questions." by Susan E. Wyse, 2012, www.snapsurveys.com.

12. "Do Others Know You Better Than You Know Yourself?" by Joachim Krueger, Ph.D., 2012, www.psychologytoday.com.

13. "The Tale of Two Brains." a DVD by Mark Gungor, www.markgungor.com.

14. "Male and Female Brains are Wired Differently Study." by AFP Relax News, 2013, www.nydailynews.com.

15. The Scientific Flaws of Online Dating Sites." by Eli J. Finkel, Susan Sprecher, 2012. www.scientificamerican.com.

16. "50 Proven Tips for Making Your Marriage Last." by Fawn Weaver, 2013, www.happywivesclub.com.

17. "8 Crucial Things I Would Tell My Younger Self About Marriage." by Christine St. Vil, 2016, www.happywivesclub.com.

18. "The Truth About Bears in Hibernation." 2012, www.bigcat.org.

19. "Facebook Adultery Rising as People Find Long Lost Filings." by Jennifer Donelan, 2012, www.wjla.com.

20. "How Many Marriages End in Happily Ever After." by Samara O'shea, 2012, www.huffingtonpost.com.

21. "The Science Behind the Profound Power of Holding Hands." by Dignity Health, 2016, www.huffingtonpost.com.

Other great resources available at
www.tonysutherland.com

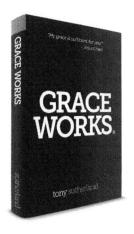
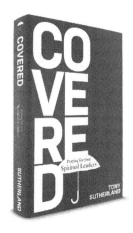

Made in the USA
Middletown, DE
04 August 2017